Uncle Bob's Big Book of Happy

(One Man Striving to Avoid Becoming
Just Another Bitter Old Fool)

by

Robert Nichols

Uncle Bob's Big Book of Happy
by Robert Nichols
Copyright ©2017 Robert Nichols

Illustrated by: Robert Nichols

Mountain Muse Publishing
P.O. Box 406
Lincoln City, OR 97367

eBook ISBN Number: 978-0-9861050-8-1
Print edition ISBN Number: 978-0-9861050-7-4

Contact Information
Robert Nichols / PO Box 406 / Lincoln City, OR 97367
MtMuse44@aol.com

MtMusePublishing.com

NOTE:
Uncle Bob's Big Book of Happy
and several other works by Robert Nichols are available as eBooks through a variety of distributors throughout the world.

Robert Nichols' published works are listed in the section,
Other Works by Robert Nichols,
at the end of this book.

Dedication

To Carol and Kristin,
whose love gives
home to my art.

Table of Contents

So... Why Me?

I should make this clear from the start. None of this is easy. The first chapter of this work starts out saying exactly that:

This will not be easy.

I tell some hard truths. Don't be misled by the mirthful lilt of my title. Uncle Bob here will do his best to help you be happy, but none of this means diddly-squat if you can't face harsher aspects of our everyday journey.

It might not even be safe. I don't know. I can't really say what is right for anyone else, sometimes even myself. As those of you who honored me by reading my book, *The Great Book of Bob*, are aware, I'm kind of a special case. I would never claim to be better than others. I just think all of us need to consciously endeavor to be a little less foolish and a lot more happy. It's something we all need to work on.

I'm sure not complaining.

I'm not hungry when I go to bed at night. How many precious beings upon this diverse planet can say that with any regularity?

I'm not cold or damp or lost to the shifting hell of homelessness this day.

I've had a good education, have had some decent jobs and career opportunities, have a reasonably strong back for an oldish fellow and can still drive a nail or a truck or whatever. I have enough at this phase of my life to afford to sit in a coffeehouse and drink $3 coffee, eat an oatmeal-raisin cookie, and expend bodily and spiritual energies fully engaged in the non-profit enterprise that is my life's work and art.

I'm not alone. Carol is my wife and ever my best friend. Kristin

1

is my daughter and ever my other best friend. My sister Nancy and all her progeny are wonderful. I have friends who are smart and funny and willing to help me with heavy lifting. I'm not alone.

So, who the hell am I, clearly blessed among humans upright upon the Earth, to preach to anyone about happiness? What do I know about the crap that brings you down when I have it all so good?

Hey, I've had every bit as much opportunity to be miserable as most of you. I could be mired by layers of debt and insecurity. I could be hungover this bright autumn morn. I could be crushed under the brutal thumbs of pitiless authority, misspent love, and oppression. I could hate myself for the sins of some allegorical Eden dwellers or the sins of my own flesh and mind. I could be miserable. Misery is an equal opportunity provider.

Here's a fast version of a sequence of happenstance and decision that describes a phase of my life. A real stickler for accuracy could point out certain flaws in this chronology, but as a concoction of approximation, it's all somewhat true to the times, the people, and yours truly.

When I had a condo, I had a mortgage and, thus, I had a job I couldn't quit. When I had a job I couldn't quit, I loved to drink beer and simulate inklings of freedom to get me through the evenings I put in between shifts at the workmill. When I spent my days at the workmill (often begun with a hangover), I had to kiss ass like all of us who don't own the workmill have to do. When I kissed ass I felt like less of a valuable and honorable person, I misspent the trust and belief of love and got my butt dumped. When my butt was dumped I said the hell with nets of obligation, sold my debt-ridden condo, worked myself out of debt (cheap apartments, beat-up old cars, Goodwill clothes etc.), moved high up into the wild mountains and lived in a tipi for five years. When I lived in my Tipi, I talked to my spirit guide Crow and to my friend Dead Jack and to his cousin God, and I laughed and wept and danced and found moon-star nights and storm-raged days and bitter-honest cold and the soul of three-chord banjo tunes and the Love of it all. When I found the Love of it all, I found my loved ones still waiting for me. And here I am.

(Of course it was never really that simple. I never did abandon any of the important elements of my life. My wife Carol remained my best friend throughout the ten-year hiatus of our vows—we kept the family love and just took a break from the rest. All of it, the jobs, the expectations of others, the journey from Condo to the mountain was more complex than needs to be told. But the gist of this progression is true. True enough that I can say, as of this day, no one in this world owes me a dime, an apology, or a moment's infusion of obligation; nor do I owe a soul in this world a dime, an apology, or an iota of my *self.* If I give you a buck, it is payment due or gift bestowed; if I speak of regret, it is honest contrition, not penitence; if I help you or comfort you or love you, it is not a debt I pay, it is a blessing I give.)

So...like so many of us, I could be owned by banks, damned by preachers, nightly drunk and daily despised by myself.

But, fortunately, I am not.

I would never be so presumptuous as to try to prescribe a course of action for anyone. My own way has been, and still is more a matter of happenstance and luck than good sense anyway. No. I won't waste your time with advice. I've got nothing here but some good tales to tell, some ideas about the ways of the world, some heart-felt good wishes for your life, dear reader. That's all.

Listen. I know that everything is bullshit until it is life-proven and believed by experience. I know that. My happiness is just that: *my* happiness. Your happiness, misery, joy or depression are all your own. I don't make claim to any of it.

I write this book in hopes that my stories, theories, blathering bilge and sublime prayers may be of help to you in avoiding the burden, the curse of bitterness. It's no fun living in a world of bitchy whiners, angry jerks, and cranky bastards.

You know what I mean.

Sincerely,
r.

3

The Mission

This will not be easy.

Happy and easy—I don't think so. Not in the world I tell. Matters profound, intimate; Cosmic and common; cruel and blissful; deeply mundane and sweetly eternal, are seldom honestly confronted without a great deal of effort. If happiness were as easy as a two-beer buzz or a Caribbean cruise, I could write this guidebook to good times in a paragraph: Pop a top, Bogart a joint, tune in the 24-hour sitcom rerun station and grin 'til we croak. AMEN. Just sit back and let our inner stupidity blather safely and snugly on in sedating credo of blah-dom and lah-de-dah *ad infinitum*.

Happiness is an art and art is never easy, never known to the resting mind, never the truth of drunken mumble or stony, far-out ritual of escape. Never "no money down—no payments until summer." Never.

Forget the *Febreze Air* Freshener! Cigars, week-old socks, and boiled cabbage actually do stink. Face the truth (change your socks, smoke outside, forbear the allure of sauerkraut, etc.) or live an empty, sickly sweet, air-freshened facade of a life.

None of what we'll confront here is easy, nor is it dull, bland, or vacuous.

For example: Death.

Oh, *The Big D!*

Oh, rattle of final air; oh, agony of final spasm;
oh, what a dismal mess, this death of flesh.
The Gods got the Grand Canyon right—
and the subtlety of smiling lips
and the sound of seas upon the rocky shore,
and rhythm and song and hot-sweet love
and cold clear snowfield mornings,

5

and child giggles
and the smooth slither of green grassy snakes
and the thunder-and-lightning thrill of storms.
Yes!

But childbirth, so painful and dangerous;
and the deathbed agony,
the indignity,
the embarrassing vulnerability
of mortal surrender—
if you ask me,
these are major screw ups
in the design department.
There is blood and trauma in birth,
and shit and writhing angst in death.
"Pressure hell! This is god-awful,"
she screams as she contorts
in contraction and presses life
through her taut and precious portal of bliss.
And when, with compassionate, surgical precision,
you shoot a sick old horse in the head,
forget the harps.
It's road apples and fart-songs, believe me.
So, where's the worth, the happiness
in these
blundering truths of stain and stench?

I'll tell you.
It's in the ache of it all. That's where. It is the undeniable,
the inevitable, the richly terrible truth of reality risked and known
and, for all the shrieking bliss of orgasm and bah-ha hilarity of
mirthful days and sob-aching sorrow of heartbreak, it is just that: It
is real. It's the deal we live with, and it is the stuff of happiness.

What Is Owed to Joy

I can play, *plink-i-ty, plunk-i-ty*, a version of Beethoven's
"Ode to Joy" from *The Ninth Symphony* on my 5-string banjo.
When this monumental work is done right, with, say, about 200

songster zealots belting from the choir, 110, give or take a dozen, prodigious masters of the fiddle, the horn, the kettle drum *et al* vibrant and blasting and banging their hearts out from the orchestra; add a quartet of world-class, big-lunged vocalists warbling mortal essence in full operatic exaltation—this amazing finale, this melodious symphonic explosion can be a life-changing moment for the passionate listener. It's what I hear as I, *plink-i-ty, plunk-i-ty*, bang away on my beat-to-hell old Vega banjo. And the whole production, whether season-crowning work of a grand orchestra or just the back porch, syncopated twang of Ol' Grinnin'-an-Pickin' Bob, is a vast expression of happiness.

So, when I walked into a room of high school students to give a talk about writing and art and such with a banjo hung over my shoulder and said, "Today we're going to kill Ludwig van Beethoven," it did garner the attention of the participants. "What's that crazy lookin' fuzzy old dude up to?" they mumbled as I carefully placed the banjo on the desk and pulled out some readings from my backpack.

Banjos are wonderful instruments, yet the brunt of many a musician's joke. (What's the difference between a banjo song and the sound of a sack of rusted door knobs and aluminum pie pans bouncing off the tail end of a junk wagon onto a concrete highway south of Texarkana? Answer: There's a difference?) But, I'll tell you something, especially those of you who look askance at this humble picker from a classical piano bench (pedestal) or down the seductive brass 'S' of a jazzy saxophone, there are few humans a-dwell upon this planet who can't help but join in on the grinnin' part of a wildly executed round of "Ol' Joe Clark" or a three-chord trip to "Cripple Creek" rung from the strings of a banjo. You just can't help yourself. You've got to smile.

Joy, you know.

So...kill Beethoven?

"Do you know," I asked the class of bright high school seniors, "Beethoven's last word?" Of course none of them did. Some, I fear, didn't even know who Beethoven was.

"It was, 'DAMN!!'" I said with great emphasis. I told the class about what a bitter life Old Ludwig led: difficult childhood, broken heart, deafness and, for a finale, a raging death.

7

"But let me tell you, none of the sorrows of his life destroyed his art. His father beat him, the love of his life left him, and then in the meanest turn of fate, this great man of music went deaf and the direct link between his art and his world was forever severed. Oh, sadness. Just look at his face—a taut mask of misery. But never, for a moment, pity this wretched mortal."

I picked up my banjo. "Ever heard his 'Ode to Joy'? Just listen to his song. He could not have created such a song if he did not feel it."

And then, *plink-i-ty, plunk-i-ty*, I began plucking the "Ode to Joy." First slowly, then faster and faster with gathering energies, I starting singing—dum, dum, dum, dum, DUM, dum, dum, dum—and they, these sophisticated suburban children of affluence and apathy, with my exuberant encouragement, joined in and the room became a celebration and the banjo a wild engine of joy.

And, just as our classroom chorus approached a crescendo of hilarious song, with a resounding slap upon the drum of my banjo, I abruptly ceased our symphony and with angst-contorted face and clenched fist shaking at the heavens, I cried, "DAMN!"

Into the stillness of that shocked moment I pondered aloud, "I wonder, what was the meaning of Beethoven's final profane exclamation?"

"Damn my life of abuse and the mad-cruel ironies of affliction."
Or...

"DAMN! What will become of this song that yet sings in my heart?"

You decide. But know his art before you curse his life.

See, it is not easy, this joy.

Speaking of fear…
Robert telling Kristin about dead
people and ghosts
in an English churchyard (child abuse?)
December, 1979

An Introduction to Fear

So much to fear.

A few years ago when confronted with the likelihood of my death in an intensive care unit, my first reaction was a feeling of relief. Though it may not seem so to the casual observer of my life, it takes a great deal of effort to be me and the idea of taking a bit of a break seemed like an easy way out of finishing the toil of my mortal days. Like now, for instance. I love writing this book but, to be perfectly honest, it isn't easy to come up with genuine cause for giddy good times in the world in which we all live. I will never intentionally deceive you, my friend. When I talk about happiness, it's the real deal. And when I talk about reality, I pull no punches. (Just wait until you read my analysis of economic reality: life in a feedlot.)

So there I was, a drugged-up, hooked-up, sorry slab of human flesh languishing away what well could have been the final moments of a good sweet life. Out in the hall, medical people mumbled with my wife Carol, while as for me, initially—as awareness of my dire condition sank in—I was just kind of grinning at the thought of taking some time off. I had artistic visions I needed to carve in wood, songs I needed to record, books to write, and blessings to drum. Much to do, and all of it critical to my being and, hopefully, of use to as many others as reach would allow. Just like it is this early afternoon in late January, clicking words upon my laptop down at the local coffeehouse; except on that September morning three years ago, I was likely going to die from some mysterious growth on my spine and its gift of blood poisoning to the whole of my physical entity.

I thought: Okay.

Then, in a cold rush that struck me with sheer terror, the reality of my imminent demise hit home. My lovely wife Carol and incredible daughter Kristin would survive without me, but, Gods know, it wouldn't be nearly so much fun for them. We sustain one another

11

in a balance of need and love and power that would stumble with the loss of any of us. Mere survival isn't the issue. Happiness is what matters in life—more than any other element of our package of physical identity, if you're not happy, you're just wasting precious time here, and likely daunting the joy of a circle of unfortunates in range of your effect.

If you are not a source of happiness to others, at least have the decency to shut the hell up.

This is a book about happiness—not as a mood, but as a critical attribute of being. This is not a sympathy card for our sniffled sorrows, this is a hard road to the bliss of facing difficult truths and still getting a kick out of life.

In that dim hospital room filled with beeping and hissing miracle medical machines, I was scared to death. No, I was scared *of* death. And that really troubled me.

Then Carol and Kristin and my sister Nancy came back into the room and made me laugh and I was really okay. I'll tell you about it in the essay.

So, I'll start this tour of glee with a chapter about fear. Fear is a real obstacle to good times. Fear is a necessary element of awareness in a big old scary world—it gives the edge we need to protect us from being gobbled up by hungry monsters and mugged by local thugs. Don't give your fear up, just learn how to manage it and still have a good life

The causes of fear are real. And, as will be discussed in a chapter called "Dimensions," there is more reality to emotion than to physical substance. Fear itself is real.

I'm not going to try to eliminate problems with ideas in this book. Problems are out there. Complications, pains, sorrows are never going to be blissfully banished. I'm just going to tell some stories,throw about some thoughts that may give insight to the skill of co-existing with difficulty.

For example, and I hope this doesn't sound too tie-dyed and hippy-esque to be taken seriously, my solution to the paralyzing potential of fear can be summed up with three simple elements: laughter, hope, and beauty. Read on, friend. You'll see.

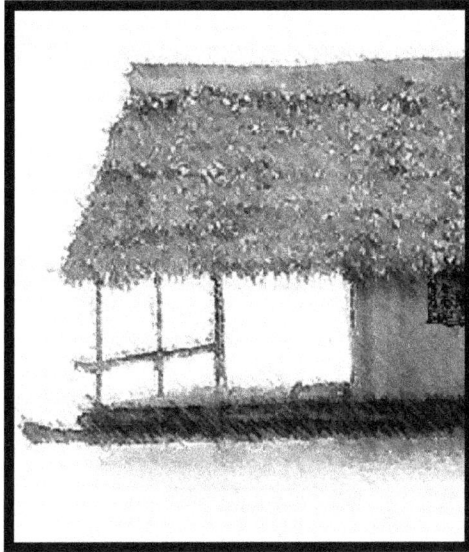

Fear
(Laughter, Hope, Beauty)

The night jungle screamed and howled and rustled. Deep in moon shadow, beasts crept through the lush deadly rainforest. I hung in my hammock, listening. We kept the fire burning all night. I knew there were snakes out there that ate men. I had seen the photos.

Earlier, in the last hour of good light, on a short trek, Sampaio tapped a log with a stick and a spider as large as my hand and fingers rushed aggressively out of its hole and right into whatever lobe of the brain stores the stuff of nightmares. We whacked great leaves with our machetes and made our passageway back toward camp where Marcus was cooking dinner. Sampaio motioned for me to stop and he pointed to a mass of bloody fur and bone. "Jaguar," he said. I nodded at the great cat's recent feast and was glad when we pressed on. What had been dense became nearly impassible. There were webs and draping mosses in the trees. There was, ever in the intense heat and moisture, a tinge of rot to the air. I couldn't see the birds. They did not sing, they screeched. I glanced behind and saw the vegetation had folded upon itself and erased all sign of our passing. When I looked back, Sampaio was gone.

I stood perfectly still, listening for my guide. I didn't want to start calling out his name. Somehow, likely only in my mind, this all seemed like a test of the American tourist and I dearly did not want to fail. It was only moments, I know. But, my God, was I alone.

I have a decent sense of direction—in all my world travels I have only been truly lost in two cities: Brussels, Belgium, where logic and landmarks failed me in the labyrinthine turn of lanes and alleys; and Salinas, Kansas, where... Oh, never mind, I used to drink. A disquieting sense of disorientation had begun hours earlier when the three of us—Sampaio, the guide, Marcus, the boatman, and I, the damned fool who had paid a hundred dollars for an overnighter in the jungle—left the Amazonian eco-resort of Ariau in a power canoe and headed for solid ground. Ariau is built on pilings supporting platforms in the treetops. It was July, right at the end of rainy season and the catwalks between units were only a few feet off the river's surface. In low water, we were told, it can be 50 or 60 feet down to water level. The Rio Negro is seven miles wide during high season. We were at least an hour, maybe two, crossing open channels and cutting through breaks in the flooded treetops and then up narrower and narrower watercourses where sometimes we would have to dislodge the canoe from the tangle. I had not the slightest notion of where we were. I was completely at the mercy of these strangers to whom I had been introduced at dockside. Stepping onto dry land did little to allay a sense of absolute dependence upon the skill and kindness of my new best friends. I couldn't even ask for reassurance. Neither of them spoke English.

So there I was, so deep in the Brazilian Amazon that my karma couldn't even find me and the little Ecuadorian Indian who had hewn a tunnel into this bio-diverse madness, pissed off a major arachnid, and rung the bell at the counter of the Jaguar Café, had disappeared into the fronds. I was right on the verge of failing this man-test for country, clan, and gender—not with just a howl for help but with a sit down, sob like a sister, cry for my mama—when Sampaio called my name.

"Robert!" he shouted.

I guessed he had just stepped behind the great green curtain of the Amazon to take a leak. Man, was it good to see him when he reappeared. I wondered, "Do guys in this culture hug each other?" But, then I noticed, he wasn't smiling. He looked grave as he spoke the only English sentence I would ever hear him utter.

"Robert, we are lost."

So, what is fear? What speaks fleetingly to the nerves? What deeply grips the soul?

The nerves adjust to the moment; the soul bends the course of our existence.

Out there, alone in the South American wilds, I was afraid as in "uh-oh...what should I do?" But, also, I knew fear as in the archetypal, child-lost, vast cold void of humanity's sense of the abandonment of the Gods.

Do you know what I mean? Sure you do.

When the City was brought down with the fallen towers of 9/11, the mayor, Rudolph Giuliani, stepped up and told us what to do with the fight-or-flight panic of our nation. He helped with the nation's nerves.

When the rubble and the clouds of choking dust settled, the President told us to go shopping while the shadowy Machiavellians who actually ran the country began an ongoing manipulation of our primal fears to capitalize upon horror and chaos as assets of their power.

And, on the other end of the spectrum, Chicken-Little environmentalist have so exaggerated every man-made threat that now that the real thing is here with global warming nobody is listening.

And, of course, there is always the threat of either going to church or burning in Hell.

Regardless of motive, wielding fear as a political or religious bludgeon is obscene and, oh, so dangerous.

You see, fear is a real obstacle to joy.

But, we must accept that fear is crucial to our survival as fragile little creatures afoot upon a frightfully large and

15

dangerous plane of existence. We are mortal and we are weaker than the average monkey; we taste delicious to bears, sharks, and ants—stripped of the artificial security of guns and insecticides and USDA-approved meat, we are fur-less, claw-less, fang-less animals with naught but our much-overrated intelligence to protect us from the hunger and territorial instincts of a plethora of much more able and well-adapted fellow beasts. Fear is the psycho-mechanism that exaggerates imagined threats and thereby keeps us alert to real dangers. It has a concrete purpose, even though, easily, ninety-percent baseless.

Children know about fear. Remember the 'boogie man'? Closet monsters? Dust dragons under the bed? Remember how readily we can poke our eyes out with sticks and scissors? Fear is mighty in our mortal lives and, as children, we knew terror in shadow and myth by the loving and sadistic chiding of discipline. Think of baby's first little prayer...and if I *die* before I wake... "Good night, sleep tight; don't let the bed *bugs* bite." Death? Insects? "Sleep well my child. And, speaking of bugs, look both ways before you cross the street or you'll end up crushed like a cockroach."

So, how do we handle a reasonable amount of fear without becoming paralyzed by it?

I have no idea.

But, I do have elements to add to my true story of fear in the jungle.

Elements of survival in the face of fear.

"Robert, we are lost," my guide, Sampaio, had said to me out there in the dusky final moments of light. I was speechless. What could I say? Who would understand anyway?

Lost.

Then, a gleam of light sparked from his deep brown eyes and he grinned. I feigned rage and then such a wonderful laugh we had. No common language or common culture but a universal understanding of fear, and Sampaio's joke broke down barriers and made us friends in that understanding. Though, clearly, I had fallen fully for the standard tourist-in-the-jungle joke likely

16

inflicted by guides since the first tour ("Adam," spoke the voice of God as he showed his mud-and-blood creation around the Garden. "Adam, we are lost."), I didn't feel the least bit foolish.

It's part of the package of curiosity and fear that is the perspective of humankind. We seek the jungle; we fear its lush danger. We seek discovery; we fear being lost. We crave the Love of Gods; we fear the rejection of Gods. It is a fragile balance we maintain between daring and dread: Fragile.

So, back to the jungle. We returned to camp where, upon a rotisserie fashioned from branches and twigs, Marcus cooked the juicy essence of meat to perfection. No, it wasn't some eye-popped, victual of Amazonian rodent skewered a-writhe o'er the white heat of the campfire. It was chicken brought from the ample larder of the resort. Man, was it good, too. All a-drip and flavorful upon my chin and fingers. And there was plenty. We three human males gathered in ancient rite about the smoking core of light and heat as twilight faltered and failed and night engulfed us. Somehow, though we knew no bond of language, we managed to know together the joy of good food and easy laughter. I had joined whole-heartedly in setting up camp, carrying my share of the equipment and provisions, gathering firewood and hanging hammocks from trees. I hadn't been some pampered white-guy bwana sitting back as the natives did all the work. And I had laughed at Sampaio's terrible joke—a laugh of camaraderie and shameless admission of honest fear. It was a wonderful evening out there where nature, in all its vicious truth, suspended us in webs of primal danger and beauty. With machetes we had chopped an ample pile of dead wood, armed ourselves with powerful six-volt lanterns, and, after thorough dousings with DEET insect repellant, swung into hammocks and let the night have us.

I had dwelled in run-down apartments in the cacophonous heart of the city where car horns and sirens and gunshots and raging screams of violence and insanity were the song of the night. I had camped in stone canyons beside the roar of glacier-fed mountain rivers. I had heard Miss Quade, my 6th-grade teacher, expound upon the 'impudent and rude' behavior of my classmates. I was hardly unaccustomed to loudness. But, taken with the fear-tuned acuity of all my senses, I don't recall ever knowing such a screech of dissonant howl and scream as that night in the hammock. It was as if each of the thousands of species of exotic bugs and birds, apes and god-knows-what-other carnivores that inhabited our acre was determined to shout away the predators of night before exposing their flesh to the perils of sleep.

And then, upon some sensate connection of blood and tissue awareness, the switch was turned and a stifling, breath-daunting silence choked the night.

It was sheer terror out there for the blue-eyed gringo a-swing in a tree-bound bed of twine. So, of course, I laughed. I knew my laughter, heart-true and uninhibited, was as much a screech as any of the calls of my cousins the birds, the bugs, the apes and cats and slithering snakes and bellowing crocodiles just beyond the frail ring of campfire flutter and glow. But it felt good to laugh and Marcus and Sampaio from their opposite corners of the camp joined me in my mad and momentary glee.

Laughing at fear, or with fear—not the hysteric mirth-babble of panic, but a genuine emotive response to an emotional reality—helps. Denial has served me well over my decades of human folly and frailty. My standard approach to many of life's health, financial or personal dilemmas has been to brush off all but the most egregiously blatant hints of difficulty. I can ignore heart zaps, mega-bills, and limitation of character and worth, and just keep on keepin' on. But fear allows no such pseudo-comfort as self-deception. When fear sets in, it ceases to be a symptom and becomes in-your-face reality. So, the strategies for combating the siege of neural- and physio-panic have got to be real as well.

Like laughter. It can't be all air and ha-ha sound, it has got to start in the heart and blast its way to the surface with relish. Laughter has got to be genuine or fear will just redouble its grip on the moment.

When at death's brink a few years ago, I had no fear whatsoever of the possibility of confronting my own death. But I was honestly terrified at the thought of my daughter Kristin, with her special needs, and my wife Carol, with her absolute commitment of love, living with the emptiness of my loss. I was in severe pain from some evil mass of an inexplicable growth that had the neural core of my spine in its grasp, was near-delirious with an accompanying blood sickness that could easily take me out, and was buzzed to beat hell by the pharmaceutical wonders that were fighting the demons a-swirl within me. Kristin and Carol and my sister Nancy were all there at my hospital bed and in and out calling people. Fear and sadness were choking us all until we realized how much love and laughter were the partners of hope. Kristin and I sang an old ballad we had sung together since she was tiny about an English lord with 'daughters one, two, three,' and the song dispelled the distance worry had created between us. Nancy did some involuntary skitter of a dance or maybe she just tripped over something and she and Carol got into a fit of giggling like they hadn't known together since Hixon Junior High School. And then laughter and sweet tearful recollection flowed, and abated the force of fear as the serious surgeons consulted down the hall.

Laughter. Yes, try to remember the balm of hilarity in the face of fear.

And I laughed with the screaming jungle. And I laughed at the silence that hungered for my flesh and mind. But that wasn't all that got me through the jungle night with flesh, mind, and pride in place.

Let me tell you about an unscheduled stop and an infusion of hope that yet rounds this entire world.

It had been late afternoon when we embarked upon the expedition. The boat was a long canoe powered by a 35hp Johnson outboard. Once we passed beneath the arching footbridge at the head of the channel leading out of the Ariau compound, Marcus gassed the thing and we clipped right along. I loved it. But, like most exotic travel experiences, it was so far removed from my normal life that it failed to register as being completely real. Great white clouds rose into the blue sky and there I was a-glide upon the vast, flooded waters of the world's largest forest. It's the kind of thing you watch on educational channels. "Robert and his seasoned guide and competent boatman set out into the remote regions in search of the rare and elusive..."

Rare... what? I wondered, just what was I seeking, anyway? But, at that glorious moment skimming through a dream world, I knew my elusive prey needed no name. It only needed my full attention.

At the resort, I had been told it would be about a 30-minute boat ride to high ground where camp would be set up. After about an hour I started wondering what was going on. For some reason we weren't heading directly across the river; you know, the shortest distance to the shore. I didn't give it much thought— what did I know about navigating these waters? —until I noticed how the sun was angling for the horizon and we just kept on going downstream. This was before I had bonded and become lifelong buds with these fellows around the fire, ripping chicken and laughing at how good it was to be alive. I didn't know them and insecurities initially kept at bay by elation began to creep into my resolve. While slowing only when breaching treetop passages to parallel channels, then rushing on with what was obviously becoming a separate agenda, I thought, "Boy, are these guys going to be disappointed when they try to get a ransom for me. They're out of luck unless they take MasterCard."

Then, right there in the middle of unending expanses of water and forest, we crossed into a bay that was spotted with floating houses. "Oh Jeez, this is where the head-shrinking, drug-crazed kidnappers live," I thought. As we approached one of the dwellings afloat upon a raft of large tree trunks—a small, square, planked structure with a narrow front porch, I saw a surly looking man leaning out the doorframe with a hammer in his right hand.

Sampaio tied the front of the boat to the porch/dock; Marcus the stern. The man in the doorway stepped out onto the porch, eyeing me. I looked inside the shack. It was dusky-dark in there. By the spill of the door light I saw a woman reclining in a hammock. Marcus entered and said something to her. She twisted her legs out of the bind of netting, shifted sideways and stood up. She glanced out at me sitting in the center of the canoe, then they disappeared into the shadows.

It all seemed tense and unfriendly to me. Dangerous. And me just a big lump of gringo in a boat without even a paddle to call my own. A world of bronzes and tans and browns and blacks—I never felt so pink in my life. And from within came muttered conversation in a strange tongue.

It was one of those moments when prayer comes to the agnostic. "Dear, God. Get me out of this one and I promise when

I get home I'll go right to Berlitz and start studying Portuguese."

Then a little girl peeked out from the darkness of the doorway and gave me a sense of hope for all the peoples of the world.

Her lovely little face was so fresh and bright, framed by swirling curls of pitch-black hair. She edged out slightly.

Amazon Child

Such a pretty dress.
Tiny bare feet on the porch.
How her brown eyes dance.

I wiggled my fingers at her and she disappeared...and reappeared...and disappeared...and reappeared...and I smiled and she smiled and then—no kidding, she stuck her tongue out at me.

I grabbed my heart, feigned injury, and flopped right over backwards.

And we giggled and giggled together—this precious mote of child-beauty on a floating house deep in the deepest of all jungles; this man, a paranoid American tourist—giggling and grinning away all xenophobic barriers to the simplest of joys.

The father, kneeling at the end of the porch nailing down loose boards, broke the serious surface demeanor of his culture and nodded a smile at me. The mother's laugher burst from inside and Marcus emerged with a pack of cigarettes in his hand. Sampaio smiled back at me and said something like, "Cigarettos." And out loud, I laughed and said, "Wow, this is an Amazonian version of a 7-11!"

As we pulled away, the mother in the sunlight, sensually soft; the father, lean and angular; and the beautiful little girl, sparkling with life and fun: they all waved.

Yes, the little girl who saved the world from fear.

And the night never lost its frightful edge. I thought it was just me—scared giddy and too nervous to sleep; weary and wishing slumber would take me to sunrise; vibrantly alive and alert with wild-eyed wonder at the fragile truth of the mortal

21

moment. I thought I was the only conscious camper in the woods until, with a swish and snap, something stirred high in the great trees. In an instant, from three corners of the campsite, six-volt spotlight beams intersected in search of the source.

It was a pattern repeated with each encroachment of motion or startle of sound. And, once, sleep was shuddered by neither movement nor snap of twig. We three awoke and scanned the low-leaved shadows for the source of a stench. God, did it stink, whatever large thing it was that slithered by. Marcus grinned at me and shrugged his shoulders as he piled more wood on the fire and brightened for a few moments the circle of our safety.

And finally, deep into the creeping hours of that good night, I must have fallen off. I know I had been asleep because I was jarred to consciousness by the sound of sirens. For a second there I thought I was back home in the suburbs of Denver. "Oh," I muttered as my mind oriented itself to reality, "these aren't sirens of the city streets, it's the wail of a gazillion mosquitos. That's all."

It turns out that the most potent of DEET insect repellents was only effective for about two hours out there then the ravenous hummers just came on in for a feast. And my native companions, indigenous dwellers of the rain forest, lifelong veterans of the jungle—they were cursing and swatting just as much as I. We laughed and I cried out, "Damned mosquitos!" The forest primeval hissed with the sound of aerosol sprays.

I had humor to save me. But that wasn't all. You don't ever want to be afraid or miserable without a core of hope to sustain you. There's just no good way from here to tomorrow without hope.

And, swinging slightly in my hammock, bug spray and lantern at the ready, I thought of the little girl and the floating 7-11 back out upon the great river. The water child peeks from the shadowy doorway and saves the stranger from foolishness, and the world spins on ever subtly toward goodness.

It didn't take but a hint of light to start the day. We were up and packed and stowed and heading back out the narrow, limb-cluttered maze of a watercourse before sunrise. I didn't know why the rush, but had no complaint. I was ready for a sweet homecoming back at the lodge, a shower, and some deep sleep. Sampaio said nothing, of course. But, as we cleared the thickets and caught first sight of wide water and open sky, I discovered the reason for our haste to break out of the canopy of trees. My guide knew the allure of jungle thrill and threat, and he knew the complex net of waters, and he knew the psychology of a good joke. But, also, he knew the gift of sunrise. By sheer beauty, I was swept to near tears. The world aglow in reds and oranges and blues and grays, sky-wide to horizons, deep upon the mirror of the river, we coursed through sunrise.

And here is the marvelous irony of experience. As I leaned back upon my pack, frazzled by sleeplessness yet exhilarated by the sweep of wonder, smudged and stained though ennobled by the struggle, weary yet wide-eyed, I knew my perceptions of this quintessential moment of morning—the rising glory of the sun, the prismatic splendor of clouds, pairs of pink dolphins arcing from the surreal smoothness of the river—were enhanced, were made profoundly fantastic by the context of fear in which they were formed.

The jungle makes fear seem an exotic experience; but, of course, it is not. My story is true, but what makes it real is the universal truth it speaks. We all know fear. Fear is as close and mundane as the potential of death and pain and loss that constantly lurks the parameters of mortal existence.

I tell you of the blood-rushing night screams from the deadly forest.

You know the piercing ring of a telephone in the middle of the night.

Each day we live in this crucible of threat and challenge, beyond near-daunting throes of fear, may we grasp the richness of survival. May laughter, hope and beauty sustain us all.

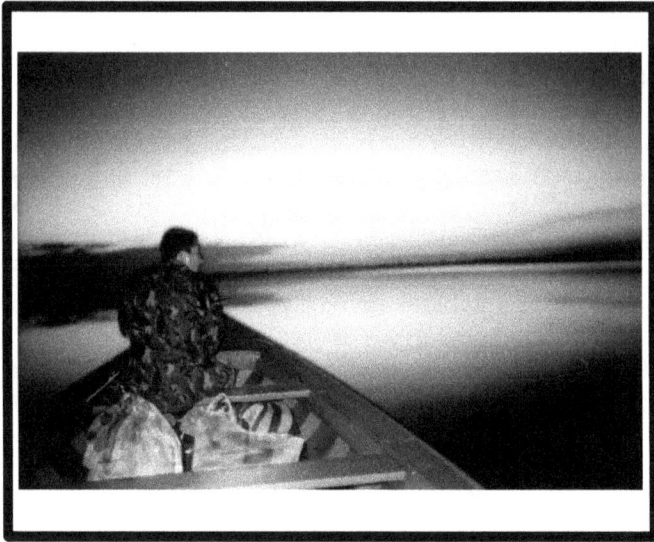

Sampaio, early morning on the Rio Negro
Amazonia, Brasil / July, 2003

Intro to Infinity

Fear manageable? Sure. Laughter, hope, and beauty, right?

Sounds good. Now we're all prepared to head out (or in?) to The Infinite.

Words are so easy to write. With a sweep of a ten-cent Bic ballpoint we materialize the mysterious and daunting depths of fear and the mysterious and daunting expanse of forever. Not bad for an Earthly lad. How about *God* or my lovely, long-passed mother? How about a full, bacon-'n'-egg breakfast right here in the middle of the Newport Public Library? Yes, words are amazingly easy to write.

But, alas, not so easy to truly materialize. You know, make real—like real bacon and real eggs and real God-sized and immortal Love. And, before you start muttering something about "why bother", I'll tell you that access to The Infinite is as close as the space between your next two breaths and as vital to you as the next breath you take—vital to your happiness.

Again, this will not be an easy idea to grasp. This is the same caveat that physicists give before telling you that your entire reality is made of a mix of vast emptiness and probability, that for every choice you make there may be millions of alternative and coexistent courses of action, that nothing exists until observed and that you have to take their word for it because it's all a big bunch of mathematical conjuration beyond the reach of those of us who struggle to keep our checkbooks balanced. They just grin and say, "Don't worry, none of this is really going to make a lot of sense in a *real world* of rocks and hockey games and mother's apple pie. Just believe our amazing proficiency at making predictions about the state of matter and energy in the universe."

Here's the problem. Mathematics and physics are not about flesh and bone and you and me. True, bombs built from mathematics and physics burnt flesh-and-bone people to ash at Hiroshima and Nagasaki. But the crux of it all is purely theoretical.

One beam of light a millionth the size of a gnat booger shows up in two places at once and the whole known universe dissolves into imponderable dimensions beyond any practical access.

So, the questions is, of course, 'Who cares?' We'd still better pay this month's electric bill or, forget light-beam wave/particles, we'll just be plain out of light altogether. We'll be in the dark.

It's pretty early in this book for me to ask for your trust, my friend, but let's give it a shot. Through wild speculation, poetic nuance, and silliness I intend to give you a real sense of your purpose in a universe beyond the petty realms of galaxies and Big Bang physics. That's all.

Come on. Take a break from stale careers and apathetic hours and take a whiff of Super-Cosmic flowers with me. Give Infinity a chance in your life.

Earth, Eagle Nebula, and the Hand of God
24" x 36" Cedar Panel
Robert Nichols / 2005

28

Infinity: We Can't Go There;
We Can Only Be There.

I read an article in *Seed* magazine that clarified a major problem I've had with science's loosely-tied bundle of truth, commencing with *The Big Bang* and terminating in the particulate happenstance and fleeting essence of what we crudely conceive of as *Now*.
Boom!

> … and then time began.
> Condensing clouds of amorphous plasm,
> eleven-dimensional fiddle strings,
> rocks made of probability;
> suns like fireworks,
> and planets like orange-hot embers
> tossed through dark-matter night
> and cooling to electrostatic clouds
> and mud rivers
> and roiling seas of fertile goo and…
>
> Hello, my name is Robert.
> I started with a big bang
> down in Florida
> back in the '40s.
> Glad to meet you.

So, call me trite when I speak a question so common as to seem cliché.
"Pardon me, Dr. Whiz-o, but what about before the *Bang*? Where did this original speck of infinitely dense stuff come from? And, who lit the fuse anyway? And, speaking of, with trees falling silently in the empty woods, when the *Bang* cut loose and created reality, who knew? Say, doesn't quantum reality require an observer to actualize?

There are plenty of answers floating about in popular tomes created for people like myself who majored in English or history or bellybutton studies. You know, "Physics for the A-Mathematical Dolt." Usually the answer, cloaked in erudition and pseudo certainty, relates some sort of circular notion such as, "Time itself began with the *Bang.*" Or, "The laws of physics themselves commenced with the *Bang.*" And, I suppose, we are to assume consciousness also commenced whenever it commenced.

"But...but...what about...?"

When confronted by an enigma, isn't it refreshingly honest when an authority simply shrugs shoulders, grins, and admits, regardless of supposed expertise, "Jeez, I dunno." There are many great scientists who, humbled by the immensity of that which they contemplate, readily shrug and smile away the delusion of an absolute grasp of things. But, there is a tendency among the spokespersons of cutting edge physics to assure us that grand unifying revelations are just beyond the brink of this day. I believe they are deceiving themselves. In fact, there is no mortal access to answers for the "big question." As my buddy Dead Jack put it in an earlier book (*The Great Book of Bob*): *Infinite questions require infinite answers.* I don't think we'll likely work out multi-billion year perplexities in three score and ten, do you?

So, when chalk-dusty wizards of physics resoundingly rap the final numerical symbol at the end of a wall-sized equation and announce, "Hence and thus and, *voilà,* so it is," I tend to begin to sputter, "...but...but."

And about that time the Intelligent Design folks, the three syllable Jah-ee-sus crowd, starts chiming in with "And-ah, the Lo-ord sayeth, 'Let there be...'"

I get a bit discouraged.

It's a good thing I meditate. Years ago I realized the Universe is just too big to explore. Some theorize that the entire life cycle of our little solar system from creation to extinction will have come and gone before light waves from the farthest edges of the Universe even get here. Time-fettered physical reality can never circumvent the tortoise-paced torpor of the speed of light and actually get out there to where *IT* is really happening—out beyond where Hubble stars bend from blue to red and existence ad libs galaxies just for laughs. Out on the Beach of Ever where Gods and Goddesses surf seas of raw essence and sunbathe in the quenching glow of Super-Conscious Love.

Maybe thirty years ago, I began developing techniques of spirit journey based upon simultaneity rather than distance. You should try it sometime. It's not easy but worth the effort. The hardest part is freeing yourself of notions of a concrete, visual image of a timeless concept of *ALL*. It really can't work. Time is one of the three components of the most basic formula learned in high school physics.

$$\underline{D}\text{istance} = \underline{V}\text{elocity } \textit{times } \underline{T}\text{ime}$$

Eliminate time from the equation and both velocity and distance just collapse and a spatial construct of simultaneous interaction with the Universe is unimaginable. (Just like the ten or eleven dimensions string theorists propose—talk about mental contortion. You've got your up-'n'-down, side to side, in-'n'-out, and time of day. That's all just fine, but then they want you to start adding spirals and edges and rings around the where'd-it-go and you're lucky if you ever get your eyes uncrossed again.)

So, simultaneity can't be seen. But don't despair. It can be symbolically experienced through the wonder of poetry. That's right. I said *poetry*.

If we accept the metaphoric nature of supposed reality and treat images and sounds and all the other data collected by our various senses as mediums used in the expression of a wild and wonderful array of art, our normal means of expressing concept can serve us well. Once the rock-and-river of the Grand Canyon becomes a visionary portal to exquisite swirls of sentiment and awe; once love ceases to be but transient flesh upon flesh and becomes giddy-sweet delight; once sunrise transcends from optical/meteorological phenomenon and glows as glorious prayer of a brand new day—then let the magic show begin.

In the fifth level of my meditation (that is 5th of 6, with Six being open interaction with Universal Consciousness) I deal with the transition beyond the physics of *The Big Bang* and its sluggish arrow of time by experiencing the symbolic absorption of the Cosmos. I begin with the whirring caress of Earth itself spinning within my chest, and once the Milky Way has spiraled into the core of my heart and the rest of the stardust, blaze, fusion and fury of the seen, unseen and unfathomable night are a-whirl within my breast, I'm really getting out to where motion becomes emotion and existence a lovely song sung like gentle laughter and spilled hot like joyous tears.

You can imagine my pleasure in reading in *Seed* magazine an article by cosmologist Sean Carroll that relates a theory he and Jennifer Chen are advancing that *The Big Bang* is but a blip on the screen of Ever. A quirk, a hiccup in which we are entrapped by the physics of entropy and its inherent time so deeply embedded in the mire of gas-blasted galaxies as to have only religious notions of Gods. A blip upon the field of an infinite Super Reality so far beyond the reach of our petty hours and squinting telescopes as to seem non-existent.

Non-existent? Nonsense! I've been there.

And then, talk about serendipity, just as I was writing these lines that afternoon, my good friend Arthur Knebel called. Arthur was an artist, musician, philosopher, and dear friend. He had been playing a work by Bach on his viola and called to say that it contained passages so sublime that as he played them, in the lapse of a 16th note there expanded within him a sense of timelessness vastly beyond the crude approximation of hours. Over the decades of his music, he had repeatedly experienced such suspensions of temporal/mortal limitation. I said, "Funny thing, Arthur, I was just writing about that this morning." I knew exactly what he was describing. So would Sean Carroll and Jennifer Chen. And, probably, so do you. I suspect that many of us have such inklings of realms beyond the rigid reality of rational science. It's just not the kind of thing one drops into the shallow waters of casual conversation—the notion that our entire cosmos may well just be a speck floating across one of the million eyes of a minor God.

I'll give you a poet's report from the outer edge of this aberrant fizzle and fling of Big Bang phenomena. I traveled there in simultaneous meditation last week.

It's about stillness, you know.

Stillness. The Dalai Lama says we should meditate upon our own consciousness in a state free from past memory or future notion.

Suspended, it would seem, in an immovable *Now*.

However, there is no such a thing as 'immovable" in the reality envisioned by science. The nature of our observable universe is one of absolute, ubiquitous motion. Not an ion or quark or string or Himalayan peak is ever at rest. Not a point exists in all the whirl and sprawl of *The Big Bang* universe where motion ceases. Whether measured by entropy, celestial spin, or rattle-ring of this morning's alarm clock—the great pendulum never ceases to swing. Once time was created, it became forever restless.

Therefore, the absolute stillness of *Now* must exist external to the physical reality of hours and galaxies: out in the infinite, eternal essence—the timeless matrix upon which dabble the petty destinies of universes.

Okay. I'll take you there via, I admit, a bit of a dramatization. But true of essence. All true. Remember, it is only the marvelous poetic approximation of metaphor that indeed speaks reality.

It began with morning meditation in my living room. From the bridge of my Starship La-Z-Boy Recliner, the known universe spun about me...and then within me...and...picture me there, a solitary man standing upon the jutting prominence of eon-cooled matter, hair a-stream behind me, eyes intent as I peer into the mystery. Well, actually, it was more like a grassy knoll, and most of my best hairs blew away years ago. And I wasn't even alone. I was greeted there by a tour-guide God who said I could call him Bob.

"Bob?" I asked. "But, that's *my* name."

"I know."

"Oh."

Yes, a green grassy hillock falling away to an endless and unmoving cardboard sea.

In near-queasy disbelief, I sputtered to God, "It's...it's beige and just tiers and tiers of cardboard disks with gear-like edges. This is the Great Beyond?"

"Yep."

"Beige?"

You should have heard the gentle roar of his quiet laughter. "You don't like beige?"

"But I've come so far."

"Not really, Bob. But that's not important. What matters is you realize you are here. And, don't worry about what you believe you are seeing. It's how *We* store that which is not comprehensible in the scope of your perceptual dimensions."

"Huh?"

"These *wheels* are actually a kind of Super Cosmic joke. Spin them and they crystallize into the stillness and energy of hyper-galactic flowers."

"Flowers. I'd like to see that, Mr. Bob God."

"I'm sure you would. However, I must caution you. You are mortal and, at present, lack the capacity for grasping the tactile emanations of the super-spectral colors of such a song. Any more than the most infinitesimal glimpse, and you could be tickled to death instantly."

"I can think of worse ways to go."

"Better than being bored to death, right?"

"You've got that right. Come on, give me a shot at the Big Bouquet. I'm tougher than you may know."

The Deity, who looked disturbingly like me, said, "I'm really impressed. You're willing to risk death for what will be, in effect, but a glimpse of the Ultimate Aesthetic."

"Well...I really would rather not die. I'd like to have some good old-fashioned mortal time to contemplate the Glimpse. You know, maybe share it in a poem or strum it on my guitar."

"I see. Well, perhaps I did somewhat exaggerate the perils. 'Tickled to death' is a bit strong. Tickled to transformation might say it better. Yes, you merely risk permanent alteration of your entire being."

"Is this what happened to Vincent van Gogh right before he sliced off an ear?"

"That fellow sure had a way with paint, didn't he?"

"Let's get on with it, Holy One. Somewhere back on the old home planet this meditation is surely running out of *oms*. I'm ready! Turn on the lights!"

"All right. But just one more caveat. Your physicists define the arrow of time as a movement from low to high entropy."

"Yes. From order toward chaos."

"Wrong-o, Earth fellow. From tight-assed to uninhibited! So far, in the existence of your little universe, this journey from *The Big Bang* has taken all the 'time' that has ever existed. And now on this mini-fleck of a mortal moment you want to see beyond the local occlusion of The Big Bang Light Show and experience the Super-Mama of All? Is that right?"

"To quote you, Mr. God, 'Yep.'"

"Okay. The Gods admire a good fool. Are you ready?"

"Ready!"

"You realize, of course, that this too is an illusion and what you are about to experience has nothing to do with flowers, colors, sounds or anything else for which you have concept, much less, vocabulary."

"What do you mean?"

"I mean, I don't need to swear you to secrecy. The best you'll ever utter about this will be pure blather."

"Oh. That's no problem. I used to drink. My friends are accustomed to my drivel."

35

"Take a last look, My Friend. It will never be the same again."

I looked back and there, from this timeless realm, suspended like an instant of shattering glass, was the 13½ billion-year spectacle of all the universe observed and projected and theorized by humankind.

"Let's do it!" I shouted.

"Here goes. This will be quick and can only register in your minute consciousness as poetry suspended by emotion, but here goes."

God walked down a stone path to the outer edge of the Cosmos, reached out, and like a contestant on *Wheel of Fortune,* gave the closest cardboard disk a hearty spin.

Poet that I am, I think I said, "Wow!"

"Was it good for you?"

"Why am I laughing and crying?"

"Good, yes?"

"Oh, yes. I'd say it's good. Such an exquisite ache this is."

"Yes. And…?"

"I think I've been here before."

"The epiphany of hilarity and love? Prelude to a kiss? A sip from the Buddha's chalice of compassion?"

"Yes, yes… The certain, magical magnetism of an impending kiss, the warmth of knowing a gift is received, and such a delightful ache to laugh to emote to weep… all this and, also, it's kind of like a wonderful old song."

"A sense of the collective Soul of all Being singing in the Chorus of Ever?"

"Yes, yes…something like that. These feelings…I know these feelings. These emotions are so real!"

And God and Gods and zany me and the whole Chorus of Ever, how we laughed, how we sang, how we wept, how we existed.

And a God called Bob placed a hand upon my shoulder and said, "Welcome home, Mortal."

WHEW!

Get it?

We are but time-fettered, conscious creatures a-fly upon the bombast of a pyrotechnic instant called The Cosmos. But don't let

36

it get you down. You can transcend time and distance and know the exhilaration of infinite flowers.

"But…" you sputter. "it's so huge."

"Hey, they don't call it 'The Little Bang,' do they?"

"Billions of stars, millions of galaxies, and now you and a couple of fringe physicists tell me all this vastness is no more significant than a freckle on a gnat's ass. What am I supposed to think? I don't even feel small, I feel non-existent."

"Yes! I say. Just an *om* beyond non-existent there dwells All-Existent. You know: Stillness. But don't despair, My Friend. Hang on, this is not intended to be an exercise in insignificance. You are incredibly significant. You may not think so right now, but consider the odds against your identity, your particular slant on consciousness, your uniqueness existing to know this *nano peek* of a vastness beyond measure. You are alive, you are sensate, and you are clearly capable of *feeling* beyond the stars. Such experience is considerably more liberating than overwhelming. You should profoundly relish this sense of importance. Remember, it is all a grand poem and you are blessed to scan its lines with complex, scientific, artistic, spiritual and poetic awareness. This mote of consciousness called *You* is a marvelous microcosm of the absolute significance in which you exist! You are a flesh and bone, wind-ravaged and love-caressed wonder of consciousness suspended by an infinity beyond the stellar heavens."

Oh, these precious mortal lives we live. This rich, fleeting, and local sojourn in time. With flesh, spirit, mind, and heart we are blessed to exist simultaneously in realms of rock and passion and time, and realms of stillness and eternity.

Not bad, huh?

Intro to the Dreaded Finite

Just a few words of preparation before diving right into some of the most difficult material in this work. Not *difficult* like long division; *difficult* like hard to deal with without getting really pissed off.

In my little book, *Summer Words, 2000*, I included an essay on seriousness. I think it might give some helpful perspective on our encounter with the finite. It's short. I'll reprint it here. Hey, there have to be some advantages to owning the publishing house.

A Serious Problem

I don't believe life should ever be taken seriously.

I realize this all can be dismissed as a matter of semantics so I'd better clarify my application of the word, serious. I'm not saying "serious" as opposed to "frivolous." There is nothing frivolous about this process—from the quenching delight of each breath of air that sustains life to the vital taste of food that maintains energy to the fantastic touch of carnal embrace that procreates our species. And when air is given flight in laughter, and food is given art in flavor, and sex is given bliss in love—we're talking profound existence.

I'm opposing "serious" with such significant antonyms as humorous, light, emotive, pleasurable—human.

Serious people don't cry at funerals or weddings, and they don't laugh when they pray or make love.

See what I mean? The word "serious" is but a semantic choice; however, the concept is as deep as the meaning of our lives.

I know devoutly religious people who speak of the love of God and don't even crack a smile. I know musicians who play the entire keyboard of human emotions and never hear the music. I know parents who so love their children that they never show them love. Serious people are the greatest fools in the world: dangerously so. Serious folks tend to take over while the rest of us are out having a good time. They look at their great grave faces in the mirror in the morning and then go out and tell us that God's love is wrathful and create seriously flawed religions from the depths of their joyless souls. And their secular counterparts become leaders of nations and corporations proliferating a course of human history whose milestones repeatedly have been bloody wars and blights of economic duress.

Serious people: they are God-fearing not God-loving, they are tonally compulsive not melodically blessed, they are providers and protectors and never playmates.

So…

funiculi, funicula… harken, harken,
joy is in the air…

If you find me weeping, know you have found me touched by a rich blessing of sorrow or joy. And if you hear laughter coming from the bedroom, know I truly have been loved.

Get the idea? I'm attempting to prepare you for some hard truths. Sometimes looking life right in the eye can dash one's spirits. I don't want you to lose your good attitude. However, if a real basis for living with a sense of joy is to be created, it has to deal with ugly matters. It is a risk we must take.

My father had a simple line of encouragement he gave to us in times of duress. In all sincerity and with as profound a heart as any could speak, would say, "Hang in there."

So: Hang in there, dear reader. I'll meet you on the other side for a game of tag.

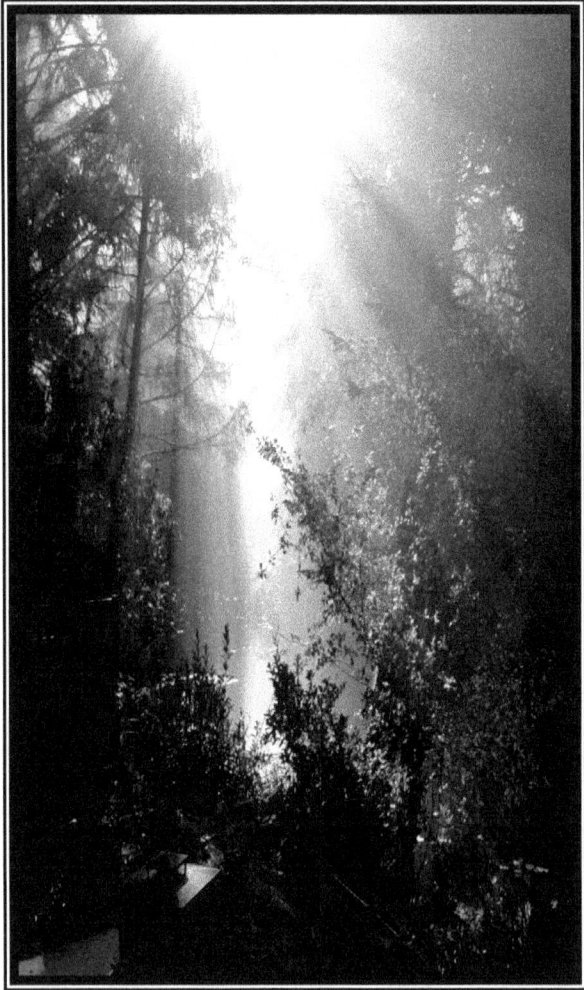

Life in the Finite

Take care, my friend. The following view of reality could prove disheartening unless taken with a proper sense of humor. The Third of the *Five Great Truths of Uncle Bob* states:

Don't blame God if you don't get the joke.

If you're not laughing every day—I mean
the sweet hilarity of kind laughter—
then you've missed the whole point of existence.

After a tour of the grim and gruesome truths of human, ecological, and spiritual exploitation, i.e. global economics; I'll assure you we'll all have a good laugh and determine that life is not nearly so bad as the numbers seem to indicate. Today, we shall not be accountants. Though we will endeavor to be realists in this assessment, at heart, we shall be poets of being, singers of a rich and joyous song of survival. It is our intention to find hope, not despair, in these harsh revelations. You'll see.

For now, forget God, Gods, and all things Infinite. Today, I speak of this world, this small planet of stone and flesh. I devoutly believe that Spirit lives on beyond our mortal struggles with potential for sweet laughter and enduring song, but upon this morning we must confront the facts of this day, not limitless promise. What does a deep-water fish know of a rainy day, or an immortal being know of death? In Eternity there is no such thing as wasting time. We of tallied breath and numbered days enjoy no such luxury. We'd better get moving. Forget Forever, what's for breakfast?

We live in a world of finite dimension, finite resource, and finite duration. This blessed day has exactly one spin through sunlight, one lapse into shadow of night and it is forever expended. In this

43

existence, encapsulated by spatial limitation and mortal atrophy, it is our narrow charge to survive. Immutably bound by quantitative substance, qualitative aspects of this temporal span are determined by the extent to which nature and human compassion distribute available resource and opportunity.

"What?"

I'll tell you 'what.' It's just like the rain.

Of Wealth and Water

When I lived in Colorado, I wrote a song about drought. One verse is:

> I come from the foothills land
> where the mountains meet the plains.
> It's been a half a dozen years
> since we've had decent rains.
> And the summer air, you can hardly bear
> with the heat and dust and all.
> I'm going up to the Northwest Coast
> and give those storms a call.

Six years of scorching summers and dust-dry winters. Damned global warming. "This is nothing to worry about," Big Energy says. "It's part of a normal cycle—let me tell you about my granddaddy and how he got through the Dust Bowl back in the '30s." Environmentalists tell us, "Normal, my ass. These are the hottest years in recorded history and it's only going to get worse if you fools don't get over your love affair with SUVs and coal-fired power plants."

And I say, "I dunno, but it sure has been hot this summer."

You see—drought, flood, or the nurturing balance of gentle showers and glowing sunlight—there is approximately the same amount of water, water-vapor, and ice a-flow or suspended about this planet as has been for the past few billion years. This is not a matter of quantity, it's a matter of distribution.

Beneath the ozone depleted skies,
as glaciers melt, the seas do rise.

Fifty thousand years ago the Ice Age solidified so much of the Earth's finite H_2O that much of the world dried up—so much, in fact, that ancient relatives of mine living in Central Africa began a migration that, thus far, has brought my bloodline as far as a small town in Oregon. (That's right—the drizzle-chilly, damp and mold-verdant marvel of the Oregon Coast. It's about as far as a person can get from the arid plains of Central Africa and I still can't seem to get enough rain.)

This Earth—from frigid peaks to arid plains, from lush forests to stark stone canyons, from stifling equatorial heat and humidity to aching polar chill—this entire planet is a wondrous garden. We dwell upon a blessing of geological and biological phenomena unique among all the sprawl of stars and planets and galaxies ever observed. Experts say this orb is about five billion years old. Thus, when you average out the weather reports for the past hundred million years or so, minor fluctuations such the Ice Age or the coming epoch of the Water Age are trifles. Believe me, Earth will survive. Now, I'm not so sure that humanity will make the cut when Mother Nature starts cleaning up her wounds. Earth's global wisdom may well deem it necessary to snuff out the human blight to save the greater being. Lewis Thomas, the biologist and philosopher, said that viruses may be the messengers of evolution—inflicting upon organisms the need to mutate or perish. To extend the metaphor, could it not be that viruses deliver deadly messages at the bidding of Gaia's immune system. (Gaia, the Greek Goddess of the Earth, is a name used to refer to a hypothesis proposed by James Lovelock that the Earth can be viewed as functioning as one huge living organism.) As, with the hubris of divine delusion, we 'stewards of the Earth' plunder the wondrous plenty of this garden for the fleeting pleasure of today's sate, I fear the grander entity of an entire planet may well be devising deadly attacks upon humankind in defense of a massive and delicate balance sustaining the eons instead of the priorities of ExxonMobil's profit projections.

As I write today I realize microorganisms are likely conspiring to evolve systems to counter the horrific damage our human

45

infestation does to Gaia. It is conceivable that Earth may be best served by ridding herself of the curse of *Homo sapiens*. While I would certainly understand such a reaction, wouldn't it be a shame for us to be eradicated after all the struggle it took to get us this far?

Swine flu, anyone?

I'm an old English major who has breached the cryptic mysteries of physics only in the last decade with books of the ilk of *The Tao of Physics, The Dancing Wu Li Masters, A Brief History of Time, The Elegant Universe.* I don't claim to have grasped the entirety of any of these readings, but I am a better poet for the encounters. You see, as a child of the Age of the Bomb, while rolled in a fetal ball beneath my desk in Miss Kramer's 4th-grade classroom and trying vainly to stifle the giggles (we all knew it was ridiculous to think we could hide from massive roils of radiation), I came to the conclusion that science was the enemy of goodness and security. Over a half century later and I'm still a bit skeptical.

But I don't despair. It is at this point in the turn of times that we of art and science must meld into the higher beings who may save us all. Living organisms, as culminations of all histories leading to this moment, are sentient bodies of experience. We humans sustain, in varying degrees of awareness, an existence rich in biophysical reality, marvelously mired in primordial essence and, simultaneously—when unfettered from the tissue of our mortal bounds—conceptually and spiritually abundant. What a deal! How do we dare to take such a blessing of earthly delight and Cosmic energy and make such a mess of things?

Here's how I put it together. Life is the aggressive pursuit and reservoir of experience; humanity's distinction among species is defined by sophistication of communication; therefore, art, as the pinnacle of communicated human experience, is the highest expression of our evolution. That which is artful in each of us, is the best of our world. I don't mean the egomaniacal atrocities of the past century, the mumbling of marginally talented fools with cacophonous visions of their own inadequacy. I mean Michelangelo's Sistine fingertips reaching for God, I mean the stretching metaphor of near-dissonance subtly vibrant in the tones of Pachelbel's *Canon*, I mean the corny sadness of "You Are My Sunshine," the bawdy-fierce, flawed humanity of Shakespeare and

Dylan Thomas. I mean the poetry of Einstein's physics and science of van Gogh's sunflowers. As complex as quantum physics, as heartfelt as poetry, and as basic as the intricacy of eloquent human interaction—I mean art as connection and connection as synthesis and synthesis as further evolution. Art as the mutating outer edge of human development and adaptation.

Scientists, poets, politicians, peddlers and preachers—we are all evolved to be artists.

And I believe we can not only save this world from ourselves, but also save ourselves in the process—as artists heeding the messages of the planet.

You see, hope is the most difficult illusion to sustain. When science becomes a careless co-conspirator with nature's arsenal of plagues and scourges to foment fatal affliction upon not-so-humble humanity, well ...I guess that's it. Blast-o, puke-o, gasp-o and gone. I want to believe our species has a shot at surviving this current rampant run of stupidity.

It's mainly about greed. We all know this. Profit-driven energy policy leads to pollution, pollution leads to environmental deterioration, a damaged ecosystem leads to a planetary repulsion of the malignancy of human folly which can result in a really bad case of the flu.

So, we need to learn to cover our mouths when we sneeze and cover our smokestacks when we generate electricity. Nothing to it, right? Sure, we can do this if it weren't for the sad truth that it's not going to happen as long as the ethos of the mightiest cultures is driven by materialism. Greed is inherent to human materialism.

Which brings us back to water. There is enough for everyone to have a good quenching drink if only it were the way of weather patterns to evenly distribute the blessing.

It isn't. Water, health, prosperity, hope—fickle commodities at best. We've just got to live with this. As artists, scientists, and responsible citizens we must do all we can to avoid exacerbation of a difficult situation by cruising to the mini-mart in tank-sized Hummers and devouring precious and finite resources as if we were the only creatures with any claim to nature's vital capital.

You know—living like there's no tomorrow. There may not be.

And water and money are so much alike.

There is sufficient wealth in this world to comfortably accommodate the basic needs of all peoples. It's always been this way. And just like the flow of life-sustaining waters, the choking want of desiccated meadows, the torrential terrors of raging storms, and the crisp rustle of drought-daunted hayfields— the capricious distribution of nature's gifts is replicated by patterns of economic capital. Historically, there has been at best a 90%:10% dispersion of plenty among the folks of the world, with 90% of the wealth going to the top 10% of the population, and the remaining 10% of the wealth being tossed out to the 90% of us with which to struggle. Also, there is an inverse proportion of work to benefit, whereby, we toiling masses who actually are out here hoeing the rows and swinging the hammers and manning the cubicles are rarely among the elite when payday comes around. The tycoons, stockholders, kings and other oligarchs who do the least, reap the most. It's the way of all existing economic systems—whether they be capitalistic, communistic, fascistic or socialistic. The track record of altruistic economics is abysmal— actually, nonexistent.

We can irrigate the deserts. We can develop less destructive sources of energy. We can learn to cherish the richness of this garden of a planet and manage its plenty with a spirit of compassion for all living creatures. It's possible...but, how likely is this to happen as long as greedy fools are allowed to hoard the wealth with an eye on the corporate bottom line instead of the general good?

How about a business model that allocates a ratio of wage earner to CEO salary more like 1:10 instead of the current American split of 1:435 (this ratio seems to worsen regularly— check down at your local food bank for the latest figures) where, for every 100 bucks you squeeze out of a day, the big boss is pocketing $43,500? (You know, while you earn enough for a quick run to the Safeway for a basket of groceries, he pockets enough to purchase a mid-range Lexus.) How about corporations dedicated to their employees, their products, and their customers rather than their stockholders? How about some fairness in this world?

Not likely, huh?

It's all as finite as a cool drink of water and as cruel as the famine-bloated image of a dying child.

Economic Compassion: The Human Feedlot

Okay, the world is "owned and operated" by greedy bastards, and that's the way it will be until they've either ruined everything (the desolate planet Mars once was a flourishing garden until a gang of Texas oil magnates took over the government for a couple of generations) or more people start listening to the Dalai Lama who says, "My religion is kindness." In the meantime, we have to live with this reality and make the best of it.

We're facing facts today. It's tough but true.

However, there is another finite reality that maintains a humanitarian "bottom line" somewhat effective in countering the crassness of the corporate bottom line.

My family and I were traveling in Scotland some years ago and, after a much difficulty, booked a room at a small and modest hotel. I think we paid something like $130 for the tiny chamber on the third floor. I was at the front desk conversing with the pleasant lady who owned the establishment. We were discussing the high cost of living in her lovely country when she began bitterly complaining about the exorbitant taxes she had to pay. "It's all these social programs they force upon us. I've got a maid here who receives welfare and free medicine and a housing allowance and child care and it all comes out of my money. It just isn't right."

I tried to be somewhat sympathetic with her complaints. I mean who likes to pay taxes? But then I asked her, "So, everything here in Edinburgh costs about twice what I'm used to paying in the U.S. Do you pay your employees twice the wages?"

"Well ..." she said, with some hesitation.

"Just how much does a maid make in this town?"

"I pay about six dollars an hour."

And, amazingly, this intelligent lady failed to make the connection between low wages and expensive social programs. Whether on payday or tax day, if businesses fail to sustain basic living expenses of their employees, they'll make up the difference one way or the other. I'm not so naive as to attribute this to social consciousness or civic responsibility. This is basic economic reality. If workers are too hungry or sick or tired to toil effectively, the bosses don't make any money. Even the most brutal slave holder knew that you could beat and errant field hand bloody, but not to death. It just wasn't good business to excessively damage the human beings he was treating like livestock.

So, regardless of greed, a minimal level of pay or food and shelter will always eventually be provided to us of the downtrodden 90%. If you don't provide your cows with at least a bare minimum of feed, they will give you no milk.

This accounts for the 10% of the world's wealth they share with the rest of us.

Heartwarming, isn't it?

In massive feedlots where, by the tens of thousands, densely dwell hamburgers on the hoof, if you can't keep cattle standing shoulder to shoulder in their shit-sloshed pens, they have no monetary worth. By USDA regulation, once an unfortunate bovine stumbles and hits the muck, it can't be used as people food.

You get the idea?

Or, as I once said to an employer some years ago when, working fifty hours a week, I could barely make the rent on a piece-of-crap trailer house, "Moo."

Of Wars and Eyes

Water as whim, wealth as greed, and life as a miserable feedlot—I'm not so sure that I like this sojourn in the nuts-and-bolts land of reality. Nature is cruel, mankind foolish, economic reality inhumane and now we must deal with the most blatantly ignorant of all human folly: War.

Historically, most wars are fought by troops either enslaved, drafted, or economically coerced from the expendable 90% for the benefit of the greed-driven 10%. (Actually a ratio of 99:1 may be more appropriate in this case—but, hey, who's counting anyway?) More recently, utilizing the ever-evolving technology of destruction, much of the devastation is accomplished by sadistic computer geeks who, sequestered in enclaves on the outskirts of Las Vegas, deliver the wrath of freedom to designated targets with guided missles and bomb-bearing drone aircraft on the other side of the world, often to the expense of our nation's soul. It's steely-cold, Marxist economic determinism that has committed the flesh-and-bone essence of legions of "our boys" or more recently, "our young persons" to march off to slaughter on a regular basis throughout history. When kings, czars, warlords, emperors, popes, presidents or venture capitalists feel the threat of losing land or investment, suddenly God or country or apple pie are in contrived jeopardy and armies amass. And, by the tragic millions, our cannon-fodder cousins of the common ilk are sacrificed in brutal rites of carnage.

Religion has proven to be one of the most effective ploys used by The Big Guys in rallying the troops for their forays into real estate acquisition. I mean, when you've got some big designs on expanding the old empire, you really need a bunch of folks willing to blindly follow your every command. I guess I was wrong. In this tour of today's truth we can't totally omit "God, Gods, and all things Infinite," specifically the dire influence of the God of the Jews/Christians/Muslims.

Huayna Picchu is a sacred mountain in Peru. As I climbed its ancient stone steps through drizzle and mist, I prayed. With open soul I sought the whispered might of the Incan God.

At the funeral of a dear lady, the old monsignor spoke a deep and profound song of sorrow and hope. I told him, as we stood in the serving line afterwards, "Most religious people merely speak of God; others, rare holy men like you, actually bring God into the church."

High upon a mountain ridge, I stood naked before the east window of my cabin as, in glorious array of pinks and purples and orange-red roil of streaking dawn, the God of Sunrises blessed me with beauty.

And again, the Dalai Lama said the all-truth to my soul with, "Kindness is my religion."

The Jews, the Christians, the Muslims, the Mormons, the Catholics, the Baptists, the Pentecostals, the Branch Davidians, the snake kissers of Appalachia, the jubilant gospel shouters, the stately Episcopalians, the hallelujah-holy-rolling-tongues-speaking tent folk, the whirling dervishes, the minaret prayer callers, the praise-the-lord preachers of a singular vision—all the descendants of Abraham are mistaken when they claim an exclusive insight into Truth.

We humans have intuited a plethora of invisible deities to worship or fear or celebrate—some good, some not so good, some horrendous. I think it is more than just coincidence that of all manifestations of supreme power acknowledged by diverse cultures about the world, one of the most influential is this angry old Jewish God of wrath, jealousy, misogyny, and revenge. What better set of attitudes could be of benefit to those who crave power and material acquisition.

In the Biblical version of history, God told Moses that his people had a divine right to move into Canaan and claim it as their *promised land*. The fact that this territory was not vacant at the time meant the Jews would have to convince indigenous populations to shuffle on off to another corner of the Mid-Eastern desert-scape. When the locals took dim view of a deed signed by Yahweh and resisted eviction, matters got violent. "And the walls came tumbling down" comes to mind. Some would call it divine will; others would call it slaughter. Regardless, the desired effect was achieved: a major real estate coup.

Joseph Campbell in his marvelous works on mythology, acknowledged the necessity of myth in human culture as a means of symbolically representing wonders beyond human comprehension. However, he called for new myths to evolve from a continuing accumulation of knowledge and insight. But why would the powers that be want to embrace a more modern, more compassionate, more enlightened figurehead of authority than the old staple of materialism, ignorance, and fear that has served them so well throughout the millennia since Abraham? What better way to keep the herds, the 90% population source of cheap labor and ready sacrifice, in control? Why risk the allure of cults of kindness when the dogma of hellfire and god-fear has been so effective in keeping wars focused and women suppressed? (I wonder if those ill-fated Sodomites were so much a bunch of sheep-lusters and dice-tossers as they were vocal agnostics and dreaded secular humanists.)

Okay, what does all this anti-religious verbiage have to do with this discussion of the futility of war?

Actually, everything.

"So what?" you say. "I don't care what other people believe. I just mind my business and they can mind their own."

If only it were so simple. Religion isn't the cause; it is the means. When the big guys determine a need, religion is a tool in their strategy to gather us damn-fool masses to do their dirty work. What better belief system than one that is associated with a God of wrath and revenge? To make this simple—enough of this rambling rant. What I'm talking about here is cultures built upon the erroneous and viciously foolish concept of *an eye for an eye.*

This devastating instance of god-sanctioned murder triggered over a hundred generations of eye-for-an-eye murders through millennia. It started with the myth of Yahweh giving the Jews a

53

Promised Land that happened to be already inhabited by the Canaanites (several tribes including forerunners of the Palestinians). The Jews acquired the land by force and instigated centuries of retribution and re-retribution *ad nauseam*. See, it's just about real estate, religion, and revenge.

And among the death-for-a-death cultures whose politics and violence threaten the entire world with chaos and destruction, there is an impossible impasse of intolerance. The Arabs and the Jews are still feuding over real estate and vengeance. Meanwhile, the Christians and Muslims are killing over belief. Muslims are allowed by their doctrine to whack the heads off of dissidents; and the Christians, by their doctrine, simply ship Jews, Muslims, and all the world's non-Christians (including the Dalai Lama, for God's sake, and, not to mention, yours truly) off to burn in hell for eternity. It doesn't make for a kinder and gentler world, does it?

There shall never be peace in a world where the concept of *an eye for an eye* has any credence.

There shall never be lasting peace as long as the vicious whims of counter-mythologies are at the beck and call of greedy rulers. Or, unfortunately, we could just look at history, do the math regarding times of war vs. times of peace for major nations and say: There will never be a lasting peace in the world as we know it.

There, that was simple, wasn't it?

Conclusion of a Potentially Depressing Assessment of Finite Truth

So, what do we make of these three revelations?

1. Water and wealth abound. It's not about resource, it's about distribution.

2. Economically speaking, most of us are but cattle in a rich man's feedlot.

3. *An eye for an eye* is a crude and stupid policy that will only foment greater and greater cycles of violence.

Karl Marx tied his harsh tenets of economic theory to basic human survival. All matters cultural and political are the result of who has the goods and who does the real work—you know, greed, inequitable distribution of resources vital to survival, and the wars that drive and maintain the unfairness with which most of us live. But it's interesting that the same Marxist philosophy that so grimly analyzes human behavior is the basis upon which I find hope for escaping the curse of materialism.

Marx probably had it right regarding economic determinism, but he and his infamous followers from Lenin, to Stalin, to Castro, to the repressive reigns of China and North Korea all have fallen short of grasping the whole enchilada. And the *laissez faire,* libertarian, venture capitalists are just as mistaken in their profit-driven tunnel vision as Karl and the crew. We've determined here that it is bad business to let people starve or perish due to exposure to the elements—killing off the livestock, so to speak. So, for most of us dwelling in lands where there are yet resources to exploit, basic survival is a given. Granted, it may not be in the style of Donald Trump but we're really talking 'basics' here. On our meager 10% we can eke by. Actually, during these historically rare times of a strong middle class, 10% buys a decent lifestyle. (This really irks The Big Guys and, hence, the significant decline of the middle class during the recent eight-year reign of George II. A land of lords and peons would be much more to their liking.)

Actually, our American, Western European middle-class slice of the Big Pie is likely considerably more than the historical tithe normally allotted to such as us. But don't rejoice at the arrival of an age of higher econo-consciousness. Our improved lot is accomplished by doling out less than 10% to the Third World slaves who toil away in sweatshop horror-shows creating the goods that stock shelves down at the local Walmart with really good deals. I'd wager it all averages out to the same cruel distribution when all the workers' wealth is divided by all the workers.

In a strictly material sense, Ol' Karl and Vladimir *et al* likely had it right: It ain't fair. If cash is your only treasure, the avaricious swine who run this show own you, my friend. Lock, stock, and barrel—sign the 'seller' line on the deed to your soul. Clock in. Clock out. Die.

And, unfortunately, this is generally the way it is. To spend our lives fighting ancient patterns of economics and society has proven to be pretty much of a waste of time. In most cases, social idealists just end up at the end of the day beat to hell and still pissed off.

Now, listen up!

Here is the most important point of all. I think the best course of action for good old everyday folk like us to take is to eke by on our given 10% and get on to the really important essences of survival for which there is no material value for these greedy bastards to glom on to.

It was another Marx, not that joyless fool Karl, who proved more influential to my development: Groucho.

That's right, Groucho Marx and his amazing brothers, Chico, Harpo, and Zeppo. *You bet your life* Groucho meant more to the burgeoning of my happy being than the stupid Commies and their drear slant on humanity. When, during Groucho's quiz show one of the contestants happened upon the 'secret word' and the silly duck dropped down with cash in its bill, I loved it. I laughed, I punched my father sitting on the couch next to me and he laughed. And, when they air those old Marx Brothers movies on TV, the jokes are decades old but the mirth is as fresh as this moment's breath that drives this day's laughter.

It's like the fleeting blessing of mortality and the risk and richness of free will.

It is up to us to live these finite days and, via life-deep choices (free will in its truest sense) determine that, though we are irrevocably tied to the harsh economic realities of material greed, we need not absolutely become their victim. In other words, we can toil away our days and collect our 10% dole from the terrible machinations of wealth and work and pay our bills, but not sell our souls in the process.

We can save our souls with love, humor, and compassion.

To our corporate controllers on payday we can mutter, "Screw moo very much." While to our lovers we may say, "Shall I compare thee to a summer's day..."

And what of Gods or God? I don't know. I believe in a vastness of love and compassion beyond written dogma. My test of Deity is simply a positive answer to the question: Does this notion of ultimate might and perception emit a grace and energy beyond the pettiness of humanity? Also, once while meditating, a deep awareness spoke to me these profound words: GOD CHARGES NO FEE. So the first time a preacher starts some shame-and-fear routine begging for cash, I know he's full of it.

Dreadful, these harsh reflections upon the way of our world, ay?

Yes, but not necessarily. Remember, it is the purpose of this tome to dissuade bitterness and cynicism. There are elements and events in our lives that transcend sad fate, greed, war and violence: smiles, laughter, loving embraces and beauty for a start. There must be if we are to survive with our humanity intact.

The Buddha, clearly one of the most amazing and inspiring human beings ever to wander this earthly realm, would meditatively meander the streets of small villages with a beggar's bowl and people would share their rice with him. This mortal who had forsaken the luxurious material life of an earthly prince for the life of an enlightened wanderer, found the path to a life of joy rather than suffering. His solution: Don't waste your time desiring things that don't make you happy. In other words, don't set yourself up for disappointment by seeking a material world of riches and power that you don't need anyway. The preachers tell you that you are a wretched sinner, pass the collection plate; the realtors tell you that you need a bigger house than you can pay for, sign the mortgage; the politicians tell you that to be safe you need another gazillion dollars' worth of defense, pay the taxes. It all costs more than you can ever afford, so you feel miserable. And the barkeep says, "Have another five-dollar beer, chump."

See?

In this finite world of twisted values and unfair fate, regardless of the chains of need draped about our weary shoulders, we need not be slaves.

A middle-aged couple wandered from the highway over to my car in a parking lot by the sea where I come to write, and he asked me if I could spare them some money. I dug into my shirt pocket and found the five-dollar bill I had set aside for tomorrow's coffee and scone. I gave it to him and asked, "Are you guys happy?" The man, unkempt with not the best of teeth, shrugged; the woman, an Indian lady of street-hardened demeanor broke out a lovely smile and, glancing at her man, said, "Yeah, we're happy."

Nobody can own that. It's a separate non-material reality beyond the greedy grasp of kings and commerce. And you don't have to drop out of the normal range of existence to know it either. You can still give them their 40-a-week and last dime in payments and yet salvage elements of your own separate reality that are not for sale. We just have to find what really matters and clasp to it. In our personal joy, our love, our heartfelt emotions—in our laughter and tears we need to honestly rebuke the fools who believe they've got us bought and paid for.

I knew a lady who lived an idyllic existence of reading, beachcombing, gardening, and volunteerism. She dwelled in a tiny RV nestled into a verdant back corner of an RV community on the Oregon Coast. She had limited retirement income but that proved to be no detriment to the quality of her life.

She and the Buddha are really on to something. She told me her secret to happiness:

1. *Want what you have.*
2. *Love yourself.*

Not bad, ay?

Such is a means of becoming immune to living with The Bank of the Big Guys holding a mortgage on our souls.

Then, perhaps, via the *poem of existence*, we may find infinite implications of the finite.

"You're IT!"
Robert Nichols / 2010

Tag

Synthesis: a dab of there and this, a dab of here and that—*voilà!* It's a new universe this morning. For a man with stardust for dandruff and feedlot for footing, what say I of hope? I have laid open the wound of truth. Now, how do I stitch these gaping realizations and bid the world to live a good life without fear of spilling the heart?

Well...there is laughter. I'm not crazy about jokes or stand-up comedians but I am a zealot for laughter and its accompanying love and loving. So, I'll tell you about a game of tag.

My wife Carol and I began our game of tag fifty-one years ago. Early this morning as I left, saying, "Sleep on, my love, I'm off to the coffee house to write the best book ever," I noted the binding wrap of bedding about her arms and seized the opportunity for easy coup. With a quick kiss I gave her a nonchalant tap on the forehead and with cocksure confidence, said, "And, by the way, you're it!"

But, damn! I hadn't noticed the free fall of sheet and blanket about her feet. As I sauntered by, she jabbed me with a darting toe to the hinder.

59

Until her retirement a few years ago, Carol was a much respected college professor. I mean she looked and lived the part thoroughly with slacks and blazer and coiffed locks and a rolling suitcase filled with important student stuff and the stride of a get-it-done professional. However, there were occasions when, as I unloaded her mobile filing cabinet from the back of the car and bade her a good and useful day, she would risk commission of the cardinal sin of tardiness to her own class as she and I parried about the parking lot with volleys of jab-and-leap and cries of "You're it!" and "Am not. You missed."

And don't get me wrong here. It's not like we were youthful and agile, lean and light-footed dancers a-swirl in some rite of ballet-like kinesthetic grace. With Carol's metal hip and my gout- and work-wrenched old joints, sometimes it's just wasn't pretty. To the passing notice of the serious and solid minded, the sight of a pair of sixty-year-olds out there playing slap-and-dart might have seemed embarrassingly bizarre. But, "Beans on the fools," I'd say.

Such seasonings of giddy fun are what make the dread realities of economics and gravity bearable. It's laughter in the rain, love in the ruins, songs sung heartily to the stifling silence. It's hope, my friend. Hope and reason for being regardless of the daunting dimensions of the universe and the crass truths of the costs of living.

Once, I told Carol I had planned out my last words. In the final moment I intend to sing out Huddie Ledbetter's best line, *Goodnight, Irene*.

She said that's all right but she had a better exit in mind. As the final breath wheezes from her lungs she intends on touching my hand, smiling up at me, and saying, "You're it."

Greeley, Colorado; c. 1978
Robert Nichols / 2008

Three Revelations: False Dreams, Disappointment, and Jubilation

Pablo Neruda said poets are too wrapped up in themselves. If I didn't think the following revelations were of greater importance than the petty perplexities of one small man, I would waste neither my time writing them nor your time reading them.

It is, I suppose, time to chronicle the events and revelations of February 21, 2006. I rarely speak of creative ideas until I have written them. Discussion tends to diffuse energy and focus. It is usually best to express thoughts via whatever communicative mode suits personal aptitude and then open up art to the world.

Usually...but for reasons that have nothing to do with technique or pattern, I've been chatting on with any who will listen about the following experiences. We'll see what's left of the crux as I let flow these words. Stay with me. At some point you'll realize this is not just my story—perhaps it is your story as well.

It began with a rejection by *Seed* magazine. *Seed* is an upbeat publication of decent delvings into current trends and discoveries of science. It was quite reasonable for them to have turned down my offering, *Bob's Big Formula: The Emergence of the Individual from the Anonymity of Infinite Potential.*

Bob's Big Formula
*The Emergence of the Individual
from The Anonymity
Of Infinite Potential*

x = the self

∞ = infinite human potential

f = limitations at birth (physical, mental, environmental, spiritual)

e = experience resulting from choices

$\rightarrow$ = the passage of time

Phase One: The conceptual human being prior to fertilization and the mitigating genetic and earthly predispositions of biological parents:

$$x = \infty$$

Phase Two: The individual at birth:

$$x = \frac{\infty}{f}$$

Phase Three: The individual as an independent, cognitive entity acting, interacting and reacting with elements of environment within the parameters of mortality:

$$x = \frac{\infty}{f \cdot e} \rightarrow \quad x = \frac{\infty}{f \cdot e^2} \rightarrow \quad x = \frac{\infty}{f \cdot e^4} \rightarrow \quad x = \frac{\infty}{f \cdot e^{16}} \rightarrow$$

$$x = \frac{\infty}{f \cdot e^{256}} \rightarrow \qquad \rightarrow / \dots \text{time just flying by} \dots / \rightarrow \quad x = \frac{\infty}{f \cdot e^z}$$

64

As infinite human potential (∞) is diminished by being divided by exponentially compounding effects of experience, the individual is formed by choices and their resultant actions.

(Note from R.: Etcetera… Etcetera… Etcetera… This went on for a few more pages of explanation and expansion. Don't worry. I don't ever take myself seriously.)

This formula is a pseudo-mathematical progression that expresses the exponential effects of experience and circumstance in limiting infinite human potential and, thus, defining the individual. No respectable journal of data/fact speculation would print such BS.—notwithstanding that the 'Big Formula' is likely inspired by Gods and hinting of encrypted cosmic Truths. I mean, this formula ends with iterations of the influence of experience on the individual approaching infinity.

Hence: the *self* equals infinite human potential divided by a sort-of, near-infinite expansion of denominating iterations of experience and the equations becomes:

$$X = \frac{\infty}{\infty} = 1$$

ONE!

…and the Buddha just winks and says, "So, what else is new?"

It really was presumptuous of a poet to intrude into realms of real math and science. The rejection was expected and, thus, only moderately devastating.

Exposure of the products of a creative life to the whims of commerce is always dangerous. Dangerous and ridiculously naive.

You see, false hope is the cruelest joke of all.

I'm really not good at handling rejection letters. This is unfortunate considering that art is the ultimate venue of rejection.

By definition, there is paradox in seeking general acceptance of matters of refined uniqueness and avant garde perspective. You'd think I would have developed some areas of thicker skin over these decades of one-line condemnation of my soul's most ardent expressions. I haven't. Actually, it has gotten worse with me over these thirty or forty years of:

> *Sorry, we have no use for your poem, story, article, novel—good luck elsewhere.*

Upon receiving such responses to the products of my heart, mind, and spirit, I just assumed I wasn't yet good enough to be published and kept working. It wasn't until the past decade or so that I realized most rejections were automatic and the works weren't even perfunctorily read, that when they were read it was likely by some basement flunky (you should read my essay "Greyhound Daze or Whatever Happened to Max Perkins" in *The Great Book of Bob*), and that without an inside track it is folly even to attempt breaching the barriers of big time culture. Pardon me if I sound bitter about this, but I am.

Or, at least I was bitter until a couple of weeks ago after the bright people over at *Seed* magazine dumped my efforts into the 'forget it' chute and, in despair, I left Denver and took a drive as far north into the face of a steadily advancing southbound winter storm as traction and resolve would allow. I drove beyond the wind scatter and ion race of the storm front, beyond the dark curl of cold snowfall, beyond the exits where reasonable drivers turned around. It was up within a few miles of the Wyoming state line—a U-Haul truck lay on its side off on the frontage road, a man stood in the snow with a cell phone, a highway patrol car sat nearby, lights flashing across the silent sheen of ice. A bright red pickup truck rested upon its roof, it looked like a child's toy top. A limousine sat frumpishly in a hay field. I could have gone on, weather seldom dissuades the call of my road, but at that intersection of wintry highway, failure, and an unwavering passion for my art, a trio of truths zapped me with a whammy that has changed my life. Upon that moment's dance of angst, art, and age, with a blast more profound than the charging force of the storm, I had a realization that nearly ceased the motion of my universe right in the middle of Interstate 25.

I suddenly knew I had lived the past 46 years of my life seeking the wrong dream.

So, I took the next exit and turned back south and on with the rest of it—my life, that is.

When I was fifteen years old, I decided to be a writer. It was at this point, by the dictates of the work ethic and materialism of my culture, I enmeshed my entire sense of identity and purpose with the concept that in time, with arduous commitment, I might eventually have something important to write and the skill with which to express crucial thoughts and observations; and, hence, and here's the greatest blunder of my life, I would receive some regard from the world. You know, like Mark Twain, John Steinbeck, Ernest Hemingway, Toni Morrison, and Tom Robbins, I'd write a joke and out there beyond the minute turn of my own small sphere, others would laugh; I'd write a sad poem and not weep alone; I'd tell a story so true and lucid in the richness of simple existence others would find a home in the world of my imagination. This was my dream/vision, my mandate, my mistake.

Near Ft. Collins I left the interstate and drove east on Colorado 14 toward Ault. The storm still hovered to the north, the highway was dry, and I sensed an appointment with destiny at the old trailer court, Meadow's Village, on the edge of Greeley. On this honest day of brutal-sad confrontation, it seemed right that the setting of the most desperate of my creative years, the times most blatantly reliant upon the elusive promise of my grand false dream, be the site of its banishment from realms of false hope.

Finding happiness in our lives regardless of the hard truths of our world has been a theme throughout this work. Well, perhaps even more importantly, we must face the truths of our own lives. Those trailer times up in Greeley were the end of the decade-and-a-half first marriage of Robert and Carol. I'll speak frankly of it here, fully realizing that being forced to confront the cruel reality of those days probably saved me from ruin, and eventually saved the love Carol and I have shared from giggling childhood to the geezing days of the present.

I recall the spring of that last year, 1980. It was toward the end of my Maytag Man phase, a time of technical toil and heavy lifting (we service techs were also utilized as major appliance delivery personnel) and hours of after-work rounds of, "What the hell, sure I'll have another beer," and evenings crammed into the tin-can hovel of a house trailer out on the east side of town near the aromatic Farr Farms Feedlot. Carol had just finished her doctorate at the University of Northern Colorado and worked for the Department of Education fifty miles south in Denver. One night, I think I was even more befouled of beer and sweat of daily grind than normal, I crawled into our sofa bed with neither shower nor the heart to bother with one and she rolled away from me. We've been best friends forever, back as kids and since and yet, and even in those empty-days, she was the best friend I could ever have. But, sensing the barrier between my repulsive malaise and her despair, I knew the marriage was over.

So, the next day, while she worked in her office across from the capitol, I cleared a half-hour lunch break from the job book of washing machine and refrigerator and microwave repairs in my appliance truck and leaned against a large old tree by a duck pond in a city park. As I nibbled some kind of burger, fries and coke combo and thought about Carol and how damned sad it would be when she cleared all her nice clothes out of our closet, I quietly wept.

I wondered for a while there if I should try to find her some help—you know, a shrink. Maybe some counseling and she'd be okay. And then, in angry spite of my gentle tears, I laughed, aloud and cruelly, and growled, "My God," and I thought of what a sinking mess of failure and apathy I had become. "The woman would be crazy not to leave me." Those days of Bob the repair guy reeked of my weakness and futility.

Yes, this, more than any era of my life, was a time when the dream of my words sustained me from utter despair.

The novel I had been writing through those years, in the early hours before work, was *The High Priest of Hallelujah*. When I sat at the kitchen table and typed those words, I was a writer, not an aimless creature toiling through humbling hours of grin-and-yes-ma'am prattle. ("I'll get those massive mildewed panties out of the water pump and have you up and washin' in a jiff.") I was a man of the Muse. I wasn't some bleary-eyed bloke of too many beers, weary and benumbed, wandering in late and disheveled in a shirt embroidered with "Bob" over the left pocket. I was a man in those mornings driven by the mandate of a wondrous dream. Carol loved the dreamer and she loved the good father I was to little Kristin, and she loved the laughter we still managed to find together. But, what could she do?

I was maybe 35 then—I'd been at the dream for twenty years and aside from a couple of poems published and forgotten, my efforts: my short stories, my essays, my poems, and my first novel, *Albatross*, had all been repeatedly rejected. No matter. I would just have to get better, to rally truth and humor and passion and sorrow into more literate parcels. The dream was not the least dissuaded by the reality. I had doubts, of course. But in those futile days, it was all that I had and it served me well.

In all my tinkering with physics, philosophy, and poetry, I have yet to even approach a credible definition of reality. The more information and ideas I shuffle, the more I am convinced my human sack of sense and synapse will never be sufficient to grasp any but the most facile of reality's many facets. Yes, I do exist... I guess. Tell, me. Do I exist? Am I a poet if no one knows my poem? Am I a singer if my song is but an airy mumble lost to the drone of traffic and the grumble of distant storm clouds? Am I real when my heart beats alone in a vast universe?

So, what of false dreams?

Hey, sometimes that's all we've got. Without the infusion of spurious vision, what hope did I have to salvage self from the despair of that harsh day in the park with back against the bark of an ancient tree and burger crumbs scattered upon a work-soiled blue shirt embroidered with "Bob"?

By damn, by proof of piling pages, I may well have been mired in self-inflicted mediocrity at that deep valley in the graph of my days, but I was a writer. And if only I would continue to work at the craft and persist in honing the art of my expression, someday...

* * * *

And it worked. The dream, I mean. Never the promise of the dream. I survived with soul intact, self-respect restored, and despair allayed—and best of all, I even, thank God, got Carol

69

back. And my novel, *The High Priest of Hallelujah,* was published, albeit two rewrites and twenty years later. Of course, few beyond the reach of my smile ever read it.

Now, just how dangerous are times to be without the parachute of an illusion to save me from the plunge of my art?

I pulled into the lane of mobile homes. Our little tincan had long been replaced by a larger, shinier tincan, but there was enough familiarity to the setting to recapture some sense of the futility of those days. The elemental interplay of vacant lot and 7-11 to the north, corn field to the east, and, worst of all, the invisible yet nearly tactile stench of the neighborhood feedlot—a sour ghost, ubiquitous and vile, still the ambient curse of the town.

It was, as I had intuited, the ideal locale for the liberation of psyche from delusion.

I stood there, letting the past flood over me. It was over twenty-five years earlier... say, 1977.

It was going to be a hot day the morning I sat on the roof of our miserable little trailer and watched the sun rising over the cornfield. The trailer, a late-fifties vintage piece of tin and thin walls, had one deluxe feature. The roof had a raised section over the living room. It provided the extra foot of headroom that may well have been the difference between maintaining a veneer of sanity and all out, wall-pounding, mime-in-a box, Marcel Marceau claustrophobia. My uncles spent decades of their lives working in coal mine shafts that were less than four feet high. That's the way I felt some dark nights walking down the hall to the bathroom.

I loved the raised ceiling in the living room. "Should we hang a hoop and shoot baskets?" I asked one evening.

It wasn't until the all-night session of talk and long-necked beers that I discovered another marvel of this mobile home architecture. The edge of the raised portion of the roof formed a bench where a man might sit and sip a lukewarm beer and quietly sing up the sun across the summer-mist morning of field and feedlot.

I was a decent drunk. Sometimes a bit rowdy or loud, sloshy and sentimental; and, of course, a blathering font of philosophy and mirth. Seldom morose and never violent. Carol, just a couple of days ago, said sometimes the most difficult part was getting me to shut up so we could get some sleep. You see, just as it is this morning of well over a dozen years of sobriety, I wanted some place to use my poetry, my words, and, back then, I suffered a drinker's delusion that Bacchus and his beer-brewing cousins actually facilitated communication. So, I drank for thirty years. No regrets. Perhaps I should have realized the folly of my ways a decade or so earlier. But, I didn't. So be it—I deeply believe, for the most part, regret is a fool's anchor to sorrow. It was amazing, though, how relieved my precious wife and daughter were when I quit the suds. I really hadn't known.

So, after hours of listening to my rambling and raving discourses on the masterful play of emotion and energy in Beethoven's concerti, the political absurdity of working people voting for the right-wing candidates who would enslave them, and giggling, lusty revelations about how much I loved the pert voluptuousness of her breasts, Carol wrenched herself from the bond of my babble, went to bed sometime deep in the early A.M., and left me alone. It must have been a Saturday because I didn't need to go to work the next day. Sometimes I drank just to prolong the night I was living with no consideration of the day ahead. I knew it was stupid, but smart hadn't worked out so well for me either. I grabbed a couple of beers and, on a whim, using the porch rail as a ladder, climbed up on the roof.

Early morning as black shifted toward gray, Greeley, Colorado, c.1977, a fool and his bottle of beer sat on the roof of his sleepy trailer home. I loved my wife and my daughter. Suicide was never an option but things certainly weren't going so well.

A few days earlier, the editor of an important magazine had called to tell me how much she liked my writing. It had been the highest 30 seconds of my entire 20-year writing career. My heart pounded in my throat, my mind opened to full vulnerability so as to relish the message. "This is it," whispered the cruel voice of hope within my mind.

"Your style, your wit, your language are marvelous ..."

"Thank you," I said.

"...but, unfortunately your article on climbing Longs Peak just isn't what we're looking for."

Oh, God. No.

"We've moved away from outdoor pieces and are focused more on Western influences on...say, fashion, or food."

Heart in throat but now not beating.

"...perhaps something on the boots you hikers were wearing."

It was so quiet up there on the roof. I could see the intersection a block north and the rote pattern of the traffic light and no traffic. There was no breeze. It smelled faintly of cow shit. I climbed down and went into the stillness where only sleep whispers and the ticking clock sounded. She slept on the Jimmy Kelley Discount Furniture hide-a-bed. So lovely she was: so close, so very far away. I listened to the sweet-sleep sigh of breath at the doorway to Kristin's room. So lovely, my child: so close, so very far away. I relieved myself in the bathroom. The thought of pissing off the roof had occurred to me, but it wouldn't have been right. I knew that. On the way back outside I grabbed a couple more beers.

The sun rose summer steamy and, with steady progression from orange smear to yellow-white glare, commenced another trek across the trailer court—mercilessly hot and bored with the view. Mary, the lady next door, stepped out onto her porch in her nightgown and, seeing me sitting up there, waved slightly, smiled, shook her head and went back in. After a while Kristin came out to see what her daddy was doing. She was seven years old. She giggled and climbed the railing. I reached down and pulled her up with me and we sat there giggling together. We even dragged the phone up with us and gave my dad a call.

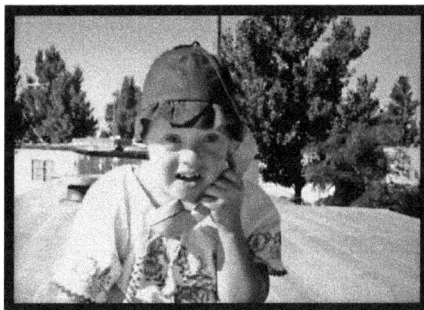

Then Carol looked up from the porch and, squinting in the sun glare with worried eyes said, "Robert, when are you coming down?"

"Now, I think."

And, loving me and knowing it to be the only right thing about me in those days, she asked, "Will you work on your book today?"

"Sure. After I sleep for a while."

It was the dream that sustained the obsession. I would write until I got it right.

The problem was, the book and the articles and poems I was writing back then (as I am still writing today) were about grand notions of the human heart and the Gods with whom we may laugh and weep and know the mortal marvel of our days. I could not invest finite energy and spirit and art writing about food and fashion, or movers and shakers, or murder or horror or screwing or movie stars or puppy dogs. Not then; not now.

So, twenty-nine years past climbing down from the roof of our miserable little trailer on that stifling summer morn, what was it I realized standing there upon that cold, snow-blown day in 2006?

I'll tell you: Three revelations.

Revelation #1

Any dream of fame and fortune associated with my art was purely delusional.

If you need proof of this assertion just answer the following question: Who the hell is Robert Nichols?

See?

It was a nearly fifty-year-old dream by the time I shuddered and muttered and finally let it go. Fifty years of a conscientious, intelligent, soulfully focused life, damned to failure by the wrong dream.   If my words are truly my measure and commercial success the gauge of art, then I have wasted my life.

Isn't that enough to take the ink right out of your Bic?

I've been a decent fellow over these years. Usually good for a laugh or a word of comfort when you need it. I can't tell you how many times I've helped friends move their dusty old furniture around. And, when I help a friend or stranger stalled along the road or a street bum desperate for a dollar, it's not out of some feigned sensibility or holy obligation. I genuinely like to help. And when I pound my sacred drums and chant my songs and bless this world, I mean it. Regardless of how this may seem, I have been extremely happy most of my days.

But, I'll tell you, my friend Arthur Knebel might be right. We artists may well be just a touch schizophrenic—as in living in a world of multiple identities.

I coexist with the people and processes of a prosaic world; while in mind and spirit, I dwell with the arching metaphor and lilting song and vicious clarity of poetry—not so much written or read—but lived. I tend to mundane matters while I silently sing bawdy, sad, and grit-true ditties with the Gods.

I know the blessing of such a full life; and yet partially live by the shallow count of culture's creed and, thus, with a constant sense of unfulfilled aspiration and its requisite sense of failure.

But, I'm not complaining here. It's the life I choose.

When I was the friendly Maytag Man, the cool and caring school teacher, or the helpful next-door neighbor out there raking leaves or shoveling snow; I wasn't faking it. I was feeling genuinely friendly, caring, and helpful. And when I smile at the tourist families as I walk the beach and earnestly speak of the weather, there is no deceit to my enthusiasm. We are all sentient wonders of nature connecting with whatever words will reach. We are deeper than we chat, believe me. You know...a bit schizoid. As for the others I may encounter, they may be opera singers, pastry chefs, or serial killers just beyond the facade of smile and greeting. As for me, within, there lives the raging, uproarious, angst-and-bliss bless-ed soul of an artist, a being so open to Cosmic Winds and local elements, so driven by the pangs of the human heart and loin as to risk sweet screeching madness at any

75

moment for the sake of knowing a single instant's glimpse of a poem.

So, when I jump into a phone booth, loosening my tie and tossing off my hat and other vestiges of daily uniform, don't expect a superhero in tights and cape to emerge. Instead, it's just me, a white-bearded silly-looking fellow in his undershorts, grinning at jokes he has shared with Cosmic Spirits and cawing crows.

"Look! Up in the sky—it's a bird, it's a plane, it's... Bob the Poet up in a tree reaching for the hand of God, laughing at the caress of leaves, and weeping with sorrows of the subtle breeze.

"Oh, yuck! It looks like he might have snagged his skivvies on a twig."

"Shameless."

Yes! Shameless.

This is who I am—a man now deficient of dreams but richly actualized by art. It's not bad except on recurrent days of doubt when dogged by the daunting question: Why?

The Gods gave me words,
they just haven't told me why yet.

It might just be a matter of the basics.

It's like eating dirt and knowing what to wish for.

If little kids aren't allowed to get out and munch some earth when they are tots, their immune systems are less likely to develop to full potential and they pay for it the rest of their lives by being less protected from certain varieties of germs *et al.* If you happened to have grown up in a household of extra vigilant mommy-daddy caregivers ("You spit out that dirt, Ashley! Chester, bring the super anti-bacterial mouthwash, I'll call the Centers for Disease Control.") and find yourself wheezing, aching, heaving your way through your third round of this season's viral delight, too bad. You could eat enough terra firma to excavate a sub-basement and the magic wouldn't work. There is a window of opportunity that opens when children are little backyard boppers and then closes for the rest of their lives. Take your dose of dirt at two or three years old or you're just chewing soil.

The point is, there are intersections of opportunity and action/inaction that can set the rest of our lives and I wonder if that doesn't also apply to dreams. I wonder if this misspent longing for fame and fortune as an artist was absent from my dreams at the stage when I affixed them to the course of my destiny. In the nascent, formative days of my affiliation with the Muses, my visions were not of a Nobel Prize in Literature or a fat-cat movie contract with Hollywood. My picture of the life of a poet was of me sitting in the back corner of a café next to a good window, thoughtfully stroking a full beard, and writing with passionate abandon the poems and stories and lessons of the good long roads I had traveled.

You know. Like I'm doing right now.

The beard has gone gray but it is wild, fuzzy and free. And the road stretching back from the doorway of this coffeehouse has come a long long way, and the road leading on from here winds on to the Infinite.

The real dream might well have come true. It was just the false aspirations of commerce and materialism imposed by culture upon my vision that have proven the root of my disappointment.

Which brings me to revelation #2.

Revelation #2

Most of my sense of failure as an artist has resulted from judging myself through the eyes of my father.

My dad loved and supported me all the days of our lives. He lived nearly 97 years and generally thought me to be a fine fellow. But I know, by the values of his worldview forged by the desperation and insecurity of the Great Depression, he saw me as a success during the phase of my life when I was a school teacher, and thought me a fool all the years after I gave it up to become a full-time writer. This was not some ugly business between the two of us. He never spoke directly of it. But I knew it to be true. What was he to answer when asked by fellow Lions Club members, "So, Bob, what does your son do?"

77

"Well...uh...he kind of writes books nobody reads and when his jalopies break down or he decides to self-publish whatever it is he writes, he calls me for money."

And true. The only way to prove he and his generation wrong would have been to defy the odds and achieve material fame and fortune.

I never did that in his times, or since.

I think what has really disappointed me with my life as an artist is not my failure to create bestsellers. It is that I failed to give my father a son to brag about in terms respected by the world in which he lived.

I really don't have an answer to this one. Perhaps some of us outgrow our ridiculous notions of parental expectation and live free of the curse of giving a damn. At 72 it doesn't look like I'm going to sever that umbilical chord, does it? And, by the way, have you?

And on to the third awareness and maybe a clearer idea of how this poet's lament may well be a version of your own story which, I think, can have a happy ending.

Revelation #3

When I strum my banjo, the Gods tap their toes.

Sometimes you just need to read your own damned books. In my novel, *God of the Poets,* and my autobiography, *The Great Book of Bob,* I tried to convey a sense of universal purpose to all sentient beings. Through our individual awareness we contribute to the super-awareness of some Grand Consciousness.

Sure, you may think, we are all part of a Mind beyond imagination, but so are slugs, gnats and the reptiles that eat them. How is this going to save a dream-busted old poet standing in the driveway of a rundown trailer court confronting ghosts of ancient failures and the prospect of his lifelong song never being sung to the world?

That's the way it was that dreary, snow-blown day on the outskirts of Greeley. Pretty bleak, but somehow cleansing as well. I wasn't empty. I was as full of the music of creativity as ever. That I had just come to realize I had no idea of what to do with it was a bit daunting. And then the revelation that made that day and all those that have followed possible came mercifully to my mind. The Gods spoke to me.

"I'll tell you what you need to do. Throw back your head and sing your heart out. Keep the words ever flowing through your soul. Greet each day with the poem of a new prayer. You're worried about not making the New York Times Bestseller List, *and forgetting that the vast laughter of the Universe resounds from your wit, the Angels of Awareness ache with the sad turns of your tales, the Grand Mystery devours the gist of each of your expressions of the patterns and perturbations of existence. It is exactly the anguished and ecstatic process of the artist that most refines the reach of humanity and, thus, most devoutly informs the wonder of the Gods."*

And, of course, this isn't the story of one lost little poet coming to realize *Someone* is listening. It is your story, too. Your poem is the unique glance you give this day. No other eyes see it as you do. No other heart beats within your own. Your step upon this path has never been trod before, nor shall it be trod again. It is your mandate to see it for all its intensity and hue, to feel it with all the passion you can bear, and to travel it as far as time and will can pursue a mortal journey.

What I Know

What I know cannot be said.
Poetry is but a hint.
Holy Writ is but a hint.
Flesh is but a hint.
Instants immortal
fill the soul with ineffable song.

With passion,
in flesh-to-dust desperation,
we seek the reaching shadows of metaphor;
and, with rhythm and sway of mutual need,
embracing in momentary synapse of meaning,
we dance upon
the sweet true soil of Earth.
Love is such a dance;
as, too, is hatred.

What I know,
what you know,
what the Gods do share...
silent smiles and shivers of fear
bespeak the intimate tangle of hearts,
mourning doves coo elegies and
sunrise is a psalm.

And I, the poet?
Fool, of course, to even risk a word—
blessed, cursed and blather-bound
to sing for you with all breath and blood
the mortal holy wonders and
infinite glimpses
a-play upon my soul.

What I know I cannot say.
But what I say of
God-whispered rustle of wind-leaf
or sigh of sea surf
or caress of smile-touch
is as true as I can speak.

November, 2007

Just a Bit of a Confession…
(Hey, I never claimed to be the Dalai Lama)

Okay. So it's not all mellow. Too bad. I hate to disappoint us but I'll tell you, I am angry.

The word ignoramus comes to mind. Or, how about thundering ignoramus. Yes.

It's not just the flocks of media-manipulated fools whose precious, God-blessed sentience is wasted on reality TV shows about homophobic duck people, farting fat women, and rat-hole dwelling psychotics. Its about the greed-blinded profiteers of Wall Street and K Street who will let the whole planet go to ruin for the sake of short-term profit. Its the fuck-'n'-run hoodies and the fuck-'n'-ignore yuppies whose abandoned babies are lost to video violence and soul-sapping drugs.

It's the shadow-evil shifters who spray-painted a swastika on the building across the street from my home last night.

It's…my God, I'm so angry today.

And just when I was going to write about meditation. I was going to share what has given me a sustained level of bliss-song, God-Blue glow, and still-to-the-core-of-the-Universe sessions of timeless mind whoopee. It all just got to me today, Friend. Really.

My big dog Jesse and I used to spend some good times down at the beach. We'd take a nice half-mile stroll and then sit in the dry sand up above the wrack-line where the high tide would scatter an edge of debris—a mix of natural sea goos, crab claws and mussel shells along with a daily deposit of the man-tossed, plastic crap-ola of the chronically careless.

And far away in some Caribbean flow of a perfect sea, an ocean liner captain nods and some aye-aye flunky flips a switch and dumps a week's worth of tourist turds into the sea—the GVP, the Gross Vacational Product of five thousand cruising five-meal-a-day consumers billows beneath the gently roiling wake of the gaudy sea-city. Damn!

I bitterly contemplate humankind as the so-called stewards of this planet. Yeah, we're supposed to believe the Old God of wrath and slave girls just gave it all to us humans to slaughter and reap and rape our guts full and then what... with a wicked roar of a laugh, does He sit back and watch while we screw up the whole friggin' garden. What a crock. Not my God—not the love of Jesus, compassion of Buddha, loving Consciousness of the Universe a-spin in the wonder of this planet.

Nature and its eloquent balances of force and breath and enzyme and hurricane; of passion and rebirth and screech and song; of dance and stumble, flood and dewdrop; of gift and toil and love and death—yes Nature will either eliminate the scourge of our evolutionary branch or, with luring beauty and catastrophic purge, teach us a new religion of coexistence and compassion.

Compassion...there it is again. I've really got to work on that today.

A boy shoots a raven from the sky with his .22 rifle and his father cheers. Did you know in the ebon stillness of a crow feather there shimmers iridescent spectra of vibrant color?

Its true. Such hues...

So maybe, in the fallen feather of a black bird there is enough proof of beauty to allay some of the poison that stifles my day.

I don't know.

And what about this wonder of meditation? What has it accomplished if the Big R lad is still obsessed with the horror show side of modern civilization? What good is it to have a half hour's sojourn in the vibe of Gods if only to return to a raging rant at the futility of a world of Holy-Hannah hypocrites and drill-baby-drill dolts and fundamentalist ostriches.

So, I'm not the Dalai Lama.

I'm still pissed off about half the time.

But... on our morning walks my little dog Molly and I take down to the sea cliff, as she sniffs about or sits patiently, I like to let fly my soul to the Pacific horizon and into the vast dome of sky above, and I sing stridently over the steady roar of the surf my meditation song:

Open heart.
Open mind.
Day begins now,
day becomes.

And even this raging day, greeting my good neighbor Chris as I passed him spraying white paint over the swastika on his garage wall, I meant the first line of my song of morning meditation. I sang the words "open heart" and I meant them. I really do open my heart to this whole madness of mankind and, with an open heart, I love most of them... I do.

So... maybe I'm not the Dalai Lama, bless him.

But I'm trying.

I guess that's what human compassion really is. Just doing our best for one another.

I'm working on it.

A Banjo Story

My sister Nancy and my parents chipped in together and bought me a used long-necked Vega banjo as a present when I graduated college in 1968. Such a gift it was, too. It's a wonderful old instrument I've hauled all over this country and half way around the world. I've leaned it against chairs and couches in countless abodes—always at the ready to launch a new day with a song or, with syncopated patterns of melody interlaced with hope, rescue a somber night from the burden of sad truth. Or, often, just to take a ten-minute ditty break and give myself relief from toil. Over these decades it's been a rare situation so bleak as to daunt the restorative energies of the Vega as a three-chord source of self-survival. Regardless of curse or discouragement, I almost always feel better after a solitary session of rhythmic escape.

I'm a decent plunker. I don't believe in hobbies and approach all my artful endeavors with passion and commitment. Though there have seldom been calls for public display, I am a professional musician even if I sound like an amateur. I play a limited collection of old-time banjo tunes and a variety of my own songs. My life's work could be expended in one extended set at a roadside tavern and then another act would have to finish the night. Old Vega and I just sing the same old songs most of the time and are pleased to know them.

There's a great music store down the road at Newport, Red Lotus Music. The owner, Evans Longshore, knows his music and knows instruments to be more than just tools of a craft. When I brought my banjo into his shop he knew by its chips and stains and the sweet report of a simple strum that it had a good long story. I asked about some simple maintenance and upkeep and he gladly agreed to pass it on to his luthier. I left it there for a week and, even playing my guitars and my backup 'el cheap-o' banjo, I missed it every day.

I came back when it was ready, touched a few strings and notes up the neck, paid him a fair price, told him to thank Dave, the repair guy, for a great job and then, man, how I wished I could just start wailing away and knock Evans right off his stool back there behind the counter. You know, explode with such fiery articulation that he would say, "Wow, Bob, you sure can pick a banjo."

But, of course, I couldn't. I'm not a performer, I'm a player. I just grinned and said so long.

I was really excited about my banjo, the way the neck had been shimmed for tone and the action evened and the ring nuts adjusted like they never had been before. I sped to a parking lot that overlooks the jetty and the surf and whole wild Pacific to the edge of sky, sat down on the stone wall facing the sea and started playing the most amazingly clear and responsive banjo in the whole singing world. With head flung back and eyes closed and nobody near by, I cut loose and, oh, how that beat-up old friend of stretched string and dingy drum sang our old tunes.

And this could have been the whole story:

Man and his banjo.
Stone wall by the raging sea.
The Gods tap their toes.

But it wasn't. In a five-minute encounter with purpose, my music transcended therapeutic personal bliss and became art.

During a moment's respite from revelry, I stretched and looked around. I was surprised to see a car parked just behind me with windows opened. The driver, a middle-aged man with a somber face spoke to me. "Sir, would you mind coming closer and playing a song for my parents? They're hard of hearing and I know they would like to hear a banjo song."

"Sure," I answered as I rose, strode over to the side of the car, and leaned to peer in. Father was in the passenger seat and Mother in the back. Clearly, they were both lost to the zombie-like curse of dementia. Oh, sadness.

"They are very old," he said. "And quite disabled."

He introduced them and I met their time-stunned, impassive faces with a smile and said, "Hello, my name is Robert."

"My dad was in World War II," the driver said.

"My father and a couple of uncles served that war," I told them. The old man might have understood. I couldn't tell.

"I'm honored to play you people a song."

Then, with 'fiery articulation' and heartfelt passion, I gave them all I could of "Cripple Creek."

Now, dear reader, if, in the course of your acculturation you have not encountered "Cripple Creek," forget your degrees in western civilization, ethnomusicology, and your Julliard master sessions with string quartets; forget your complete set of pristine Led Zeppelin vinyl; forget the blunting bludgeon of Muzak's ubiquitous hum—you've got a real deficit there in the portfolio of your life.

The wit, wisdom, and mantric marvel of "Goin' up Cripple Creek, goin' in a run; goin' up Cripple Creek to have some fun"...and "Girls on Cripple Creek, 'bout half grown, go after boys like a dog after bone..." may well provide an elusive essence vital to this lifetime's sojourn of your soul.

So, I played my heart out standing there in the parking lot overlook at Yaquina Bay Lighthouse.

"Goin' up Cripple Creek, goin' in a whirl; goin' up Cripple Creek to see my girl," I sang and then with plinky-plunky finale working up the neck for a final twang, my song was over.

89

I grinned into the car and looked past the pale, sad son and into the eyes of the parents and received such a marvelous gift. From the backseat, Mother stirred faintly and found my eyes. And Father...why the old man's face beamed in a smile and he vigorously clapped his hands.

"Thank you," said the son.

"Oh, no." I countered. "Thank you."

Forty years I had practiced for this five-minute concert.

About Weirdness

I have an essay I wrote called "About the Wolf-Faced Man and Alien Abduction." It's a strange and absolutely true story of an encounter I had with an unfortunate fellow while living up in the high mountains. He believed he had been abducted by space creatures who had murdered both of his parents, hauled him up into the sky for some serious dissection, and returned him to live out the rest of his days in physical and emotional ruin. He showed up at my camp needing help. His car had broken down and I was driving him down to a garage in the town six miles away.

"Yeah. Thanks, man. All this time and I never feel good."

"What did they do to you?" I asked, but I really didn't want to know.

"I don't know. I just remember being up in the sky and then something terrible I can't—no, I won't remember. Twenty years now, hiding, running, driving on into the night and always this sick feeling."

He looked terrible—all hollow-faced and shudder-shouldered and strung out.

"It's like being seasick all the damn time. Queasy, you know."

"Can't a doctor help you?"

And with steel-cold slash of a voice he said, "Never!"

Silence shattered the ride, then I spoke up.

"Never?" I asked.

"Can't go to a doctor. Never can go to a doctor. Doctors would look inside me and find out and then never let me go."

91

The dirt road wound down the canyon. I pushed the limits, skidding and bouncing and racing to town.

But I had to know. "Find out what?" I shouted over the rumble and roar of my old car.

He glanced over at me and with icy-calm said, "It's what the aliens did to me." And then in a panicked voice he said, "Please, man. Slow down, I'm getting sick. Damn it, I'm always sick. Slow down, please. These curves are getting to me."

"Sorry," I said as I let up and touched the brakes. "I'm just trying to get you some help with your car."

"Thanks."

He breathed deeply for a few moments and then he said coolly, "They took it all out of me. All of it. The aliens. Inside me, inside my head and guts, inside my skin—it's all just soup."

So, why do I mention this sad creepy story here in the grand sweep of this work?

Okay, unless you happen to be an alien abduction survivor yourself, what would your reaction be to someone talking about such strangeness?

Right. You'd just cautiously acknowledge the weirdness and then find yourself a different car on the subway. It's awkward, to say the least, when someone interrupts the sedate patterns of normalcy with whack-o revelations about matters absurd and disturbing. Guys like this fellow can ruin a good cocktail party.

I know. I used to be the same as most of you until, just the other morning, my old buddy and Spirit Guide Dead Jack told me, "Robert, you damned fool, you might as well be talking about alien abduction most of the time. What do you imagine sane and normal people think when, in the middle of a perfect opportunity to discuss the prospects of football futures and the wonders of weather, you blurt out some wild-eyed theory about Universal Consciousness or the poetic essence of a good bag of potato chips, or, even worse, you evoke my name as your mentor along this Cosmic Caper you call the everyday marvel of being? Yeah, Bob, just how smart is it to casually mention that you regularly talk to an old hard-rock miner who's been dead for over fifty years?

And your books. Man, they are packed full of eerie weirdness of the worst (best?) kind. Like in *The Great Book of Bob,* what's a regular person supposed to think when you tell them you actually died in December of 1999 and came back in a parallel universe vibrating just a whit's different from all of known existence? Jeez, man, what's some wildland alien abductee got on a living, breathing, blathering dead poet? Sometimes I wonder about you, Bob. And, hell's bells, I'm some kind of a ghost myself."

I thanked him for his encouragement and support.

"Hey, if you can't handle the truth, you picked the wrong Spirit Guide, Bub."

"I never picked you, Mr. Dead. You're the one who came right out of a pile of rock and a tombstone along Guanella Pass Road and told me to quit whining about figuring out the Universe. Yeah, then you told me, 'Infinite questions require infinite answers—get over it,'" and I about drove off the dirt into the trees. I remember later that afternoon. I was back up at the tipi and I was working around the place and thinking about what you had told me and then I shouted to the farthest reach of wonder, 'Who said that?' And—sure, I haven't really been certifiably sane since—literally out of the blue you spoke up and said you were the spirit of Jack Kimberly and if I didn't like that then I could just kiss your ghostly old ass."

"So...?"

"So, you've come to be as close of a good friend as I've ever had."

"Yeah... me, too."

"What?"

"You heard me."

"Yeah I did... So, to this person reading these words right now—you, my friend—am I just another haired-over old road-crazed moon hooter? Is it all 'alien abduction' to you? Or, can the sincerity with which I express these eccentric times and truths transcend reasonable dismissal and be taken to heart?"

And, Jack. Just what do you think?

"What the hell do I know. I'm just an old ghost hanging around for laughs."

"'God's cousin' you said once."

"Well, there is that."

93

You know, I think it may be time for Dead Jack to tell his own story. I'd like to hear it myself.

Near Jack Kimberly's Cabin
Geneva City, Colorado / c. 2000

Booooo

Jacob. My name is Jacob. Yeah, I know, Jack is what they all called me up in the high country back in my mortal days. And my friend Robert Nichols calls me Dead Jack—he thinks it's funny. Don't worry about it, I'm not exactly slapping knees either. I'm working on the fellow. I'll make a writer out of him someday and then maybe we'll all get his jokes. I'll tell more of this later, but, first, I'll give you a bit of background about my most recent mortal incarnation.

Details don't mean much but I'll give a few. I was born in Switzerland on July 4th, 1873. I immigrated to Park County, Colorado, via South America and San Francisco and staked out a mining claim in Geneva City, 11,000 feet up in the cold beautiful misery of the Rocky Mountains. I built a nice little cabin there and fooled with tons of rocks and traces of gold and silver for decades. I made a wage working for a big mining company when I had to. I wasn't unloved but I never did marry.

I lived a long hard life, the last few years of which I wintered at Meezie Key's Tumbling River Ranch. She and her people respected me so I must have been worth something. It was a ten-mile walk from up at Geneva City where I had my cabin and claim down to the town of Grant. Meezie's place was along the way and when I got up toward my 80's she convinced me to stay in one of her cabins rather than holing it up during the long months of snow and terrible cold. You see, I played it rough down in the town over those years, gambling and fighting and, yes, I did have to shoot a couple of men, one of them to death. But Meezie and her girls and some of the young ones who worked the dude ranch during

95

the summers saw me for more than a violent old hermit of a fool and, like I said, they thought I was of some value.

Enough. One life of many. No regrets. Well, I wish I hadn't had to kill that fellow—he was robbing me at the time and nobody really faulted me for it. I'm sorry it came to that, but no regrets, really. Regret is a great waste of time.

I died and they buried me across the road from the entry to the ranch. It's a pile of rocks and a tombstone with my name on it. A lot nicer than I had ever expected. Dead wasn't too bad. Time is a mortal's problem and I was past that stage and didn't mind just stretching out there for forty or so years until Robert started driving by on his way up to where he had his tipi camp set up on Meezie's upper ranch on Cowboy Flats. I knew who he was. When she sold the main ranch, Meezie kept an old homesteader cabin and 65 acres up the road. She and her friend/husband Dick Stacy summered there in the luxury of natural wonder undistracted by electricity and its burdensome conveniences. When Robert needed a place to move his camp one early spring, he called Meezie down in Tucson and she agreed to let him set up based on the recommendation of a mutual acquaintance. They didn't meet until that June when Meezie and Dick came back for the warm months. They hit it off right away. Meezie laughed at his jokes and he loved her stories. Dick is a scientist/philosopher and he and Robert could shoot the bull forever. They had some good summers up there, and Robert had some profound winters in his tipi at 10,000 feet up the side of a mountain in solitude and silence.

So, how do I know all this? Hey, I said I was dead, not gone. Look, the entire evolutionary process, from primordial muck to middle-aged yuppies yammering and texting on cell phones down at the local Starbucks, is coursed and roiled and vibrated by constant bombardments of supernatural phenomena.

Boooooooooooo. I'm a ghost. Get over it.

Actually, it was more a notion than a plan, this encounter with crazy friggin' Robert rumbling up the dirt road past my grave. It wasn't like the Big Guys said, "Thou shalt butt into the life of Robert Nichols." It was more like I knew the kinds of questions he was constantly wrestling with and I knew without a bit of a kick in the jeans he could waste another whole lifetime spinning around in irksome little circles. That was when I spoke up and told him about infinite questions requiring infinite answers and to move on. The damn fool just about drove right off the road.

Anyway, that's when it started. At least, in this lifetime– Robert's that is. We've been buds ever since. And, listen, you should know this. Robert isn't quite as dumb as he looks.

Some Sweet Truths of Old Friends and Death

...and then we just die.

Isn't that what it seems like sometimes? I mean you start with your amazing baby brain and a world to discover. In stages, you grow into full-fledged mortality. You love, you suffer, you wear down most of your dreams with debts and boredom. You spend your career mumbling toward retirement. You go to Hawaii for your 30th wedding anniversary and realize the dissimilarity between surfer dudes/hula girls and yourselves is the punch line of a really bad joke. And, with cruel turns and starts, people die and you learn of death. If you get to grow old, you lose your friends and loves and sometimes your children and...and then we just die.

Whew.

As Peggy Lee once sang in one of the most depressing ditties of the last century, "Is that all there is?"

Yeah, that's about it.

"Hey, Uncle Bob, that's not very happy."

Oh. Right.

Okay, that isn't 'all there is.' Not really. It's just the way it seems some days when we're weary or beat up by failure or beat down by heartbreak or just eroded by the tedium of patterns repeated. I'd be lying if I wrote this book without acknowledging such states of mind. I love my life, my family, my kayak, my banjo and guitar, my art, my works—yes, I love the art I have been granted the blessing of creating. I even think I'm a halfway handsome old dude on good days. But the twist that turns art and love and beauty against us is, the more aware we are of the blessings of days, the more we are likely to be disappointed with ourselves for wasting the gifts of life, of the Love of Gods, of the song of each new morning.

Yes, dear reader. Even giddy old Uncle Bob has days choked by emptiness, panic, and self-doubt.

99

You know...and then we just die.

So, maybe we'd better give the impending certainty of death a good clear look in the eye.

Maybe it's time for a road trip.

"Arthur didn't sound good," I told my wife Carol.

Arthur, you avid Robert readers will recall, was mentioned in the dedication of my autobiographical work, *The Great Book of Bob*. I described him as "a spirit of ageless energy dwelling in a beat-to-hell old body." I had a shorter-than-normal telephone session with him and realized that the flesh was becoming a major distraction to the spirit, regardless of how energetic it may have been. Arthur had been in bad shape throughout the eight or so years of our friendship. But, not like this. Not so daunting as to prevent him from painting and threaten the might of his violin playing. He had a good long life of art: child prodigy, distinguished career as a violinist and violist, transcendent master of oil and canvas. And then, by the worsening infirmity of old age, somedays so cursed by dizziness and core-deep misery, he was be-stilled of song and image.

"He really didn't sound good. I mean, he never speaks of matters of health and now it's necessary for him to say what's wrong because it so devastates him."

Carol, life-long friend and love, said, "You should go see him."

"You think so?"

"Sure."

"I don't know," I said. But I did know and, as a man who has not completely unpacked his suitcase since he was fifteen, it didn't take long for me to get ready.

It was late, 9:00 at night, when I left. I wanted to wake up in a rest area along I-84 in the Columbia River Gorge and that is about three hours from my home.

It's almost 1400 miles from where we live out on the coast to Denver on the edge of the Great Plains. Hundreds and hundreds of miles of this vast wild country of forest and canyon, city and village, and mostly the space between. The mountain lands and high desert open country of the American West are so damned big—you don't want to be caught out there by yourself on one of those days when your soul's on sabbatical. Even cruising through in a high-speed car, it's all dried bones and broken wagon wheels out there. If you're not up to laughing with your primal fears and knowing the companionship of wind and cloud, you had better just hop the red-eye and fly back east to visit Auntie Annie this summer. The Eastern Oregon high desert, the wastelands of Idaho and Wyoming, the frozen heights of unnamed peaks across the horizon are no place for the introspectively vulnerable.

I love these great highways, these surreal stretches of infinite perspective, these routes through the allegory of our own minds. And it's not like I'm fearless. Sometimes, in the starkness of raw wind and the bleakness of unending reaches of steely gray skies, on these road treks the whole universe turns cold and leaves me not just alone, but empty. When I was a nineteen-year-old kid out on my own hitching the whole width of this continent from Virginia to the California sea and back, there were moments of inner terror and abandonment that yet shape my soul's passing through this day. It's the road.

And this journey about which I write...old friends will die soon. I know this. We all have, at the core of our beings, an intimate awareness of the mortal certainty of death. It comes with the territory. It means life is perishable and, hence, intrinsically precious. Death isn't tragic in and of itself. It is timing that makes tragedy of the inevitable.

Death, regardless of circumstance, bestows sorrow up upon the abandoned hearts of surviving lovers, parents, children, friends.

But I did not take this trip for maudlin causes, final goodbyes, last words while minds were still intact. Yes, of course all that, but more so it was for purposes I didn't realize until the miles were memory, the embraces faint of sensation, and the emotions of farewell stowed within the fibers of my being.

I'll just tell you about it. I hope you'll see this wasn't an arduous and expensive act of pity imparted upon moribund friends. ($4.00/gallon gas @ 20 mpg = I don't even want to know.) As with the best of all experiences, what I received was far greater than I could have ever given.

Somewhere in Wyoming, I think the first rest area east of the Utah border on I-80, I awoke to sunrise and early April chill. My schedule was simple: get to Denver, call Arthur, arrange a couple of hours for an infinite connection to restore, contact other dear friends for brief encounters, get back on the road and head for home. As no one was expecting me, I really had no other time restraints other than the fact that I didn't want to be gone from home too long. I've got more to do with my life than I can ever expect to have life span to get done. Also, the days of my solitary existence are long past. The idea of untold journeys in the absence of Carol and Kristin are not right for this sweet phase of my life. Of late, more so with each turning day, I find that sunsets and songs on the radio, mom and pop cafes and storms building in the skies don't mean much if I don't have my loved ones sharing them with me. It's not insecurity or self-doubt. It's more like a thorough appreciation that art is life communicated, not a solitary pleasure.

So, I rolled over and let the morning find its own pace. I sleep better in a good reclining car seat than any bed I know. I was warm, alive and on a mission. And, man, was I on the road.

About 8:00 I made a run to the facilities, washed away the night, returned to the car and sat there in the marvelous stillness of deep meditation for a timeless hour. It is all so rich as breath becomes subtle soul caress and out of invisible wonder essence of Love is known. There is purpose to all this—all we sense, all we touch, and all we feel. Purpose in living; purpose in a Wyoming morning on a road-trip stanza of a good long poem.

For those of you who have never traveled this stretch of highway, or have traveled it and intentionally erased it from conscious recall, let me describe what the day's travel portended. From border to border, the southern width of Wyoming from Utah to Nebraska requires considerable patience and a heightened sense of the worth of earth-tone texture, rock bluffs, and stark vegetation to be perceived as more than a torturous long trek through wasteland. The wind is fierce, the heat in the summer and cold in the winter are intense, the towns are the raw-edged settlements of various enterprises of extractive commerce. The people you meet are a fine bunch unless you let slip that you're a card-carrying Communist or even just a registered Democrat. I mean, the Federal office building in Casper is named after Dick Cheney. But, for me, it is the rough edge of a facet of nature that

102

is beautiful in its hostility, challenging in its unapologetic coarseness. And the good folks of this state, with the exception of the miserable, white supremacist assholes, are no bunch of lap-cat liberals, they are barn-cat Republicans. I have to admire that, even if I think they've got their politics all screwed up.

The Wyoming to which I awoke that clear cool-road morning was vast and told by stone and dry wash and the desiccated pale green starkness of sage flora. The rest area was clean. Even if road hogs had littered the place, trash was long gone—carried south toward Colorado by the incessant wind. Except for wind sound, it was a quiet place. The trucks parked there actually shut down their diesel engines.

But don't despair, self-feeders, once the gusts are braved, there is safe haven for you hardy folk to picnic your little vegetarian stomachs full. The Federal/State authorities have constructed three-sided concrete shelters with stone-slab tables and benches. Perfect abodes for a miserable meal alee of the howling breath of Boreas. As for me, I made better use of one of the structures and saved my appetite for more comfortable accommodations and truck-stop waitresses who call you "Honey." Forget the wicker picnic kit, I grabbed my old Vega banjo, took a seat on the tabletop, and cut loose with some "Cripple Creek" and "Old Joe Clark," and a few of my own plunk-wild ditties and songs of life.

Days upon the highway,
nights upon the road
make me stop and wonder why.
Then there're mornings full of sunshine,
evenings by a stream,
and stars a-spinning mysteries
in the sky.

(If you'd like to see a video of your truly plunking this tune, go to:
Youtube.com
Robert Nichols Road Song / Old Route 66
https://www.youtube.com/watch?v=-IXPzpDZXx8)

The acoustics were superb.

It's interesting. Arthur, dear friend that he was, with his incredible ear and sophisticated, lifelong commitment to classical music, was incapable of abiding even the most fleeting mention of my banjo music—much less possessing the tolerance to listen to it. I made sure to offer to twang down a tune or two for him every time we met just to watch him squirm. Soul-friends aren't necessarily products of the same passions.

It's all about timing, this song/poem of life. Like airliners circling a terminal awaiting clearance for safe landing, we pace ourselves on the journey. Guided by intuitions and other mysteries, we are wise to heed the internal mechanisms of our consciousness and not force the rhythms of our intersections with fate. Karma knows. Listen and act accordingly.

So, instead of efficiently roaring out of the rest area and careening at 75 mph eastward toward my objective in Denver, I just sat there in the picnic shelter and played my banjo while the wind and sun went about their missions of motion and energy. There is a place for each of us in this process. As I said, the acoustics were great.

Timing, pacing, the intricate weaving of destinies, the happenstance of serendipity, the counterpoint of complex interactions of life stories, blind luck, Divine intervention—who can say? But, I'll tell you, my friend, when I finally quit banging on the old banjo and made my way across the hundreds of miles via the expenditure of most of another day to Denver, I arrived in alignment with the will of Gods.

I found Arthur, terribly frail of flesh, yet mighty of spirit. The three of us, skinny old Arthur, lovely Susan, and just me, how we laughed. And how deeply we conversed about the nature of art and the tales of our lives. And how we cringed through volley rounds of bad puns. And then, though nearly exhausted by the energies cast into the fray of intellectual and artful encounter, Arthur bestowed his gift upon me. He cautiously arose from his chair and picked up his violin from atop Susan's piano. When he was in better repair, it was a marvel to see him play. As he would set himself for the performance, a physical transformation would occur. A tall and nearly gaunt figure, he would rise to a posture and stance of such solidity as to be mighty. Stalwart, transfixed in focus, and with delicate balance of passion and perfection—oh, such music he played.

Sometimes, it seems, we become but shadows of our own destinies. Violin in hand, he unsteadily turned to Susan and I, leaned back into the curve of the grand Steinway, and grinning, said, "If I don't lean against this damned piano, I'll fall over."

And then, my God—the music. He placed the instrument beneath his chin, lifted the bow, and commenced to engulf me in immortal beauty.

I should tell you a story of sorrow and resolution that is at the core of what I had to share with my friends who were in mortal peril. I'll make this brief. We all know parts of this tale.

My great nephew Michael Virgin is dead and the void of his loss is as permanent as the indelible imprint of his amazing being upon the individual and collective memories of all who knew him. Tall and Greek-God beautiful and smart and kind and human and frail and human and strong, the boy was just 21 when he broke his neck. Actually, it was the night of his 21st birthday, after a day of sky diving, bungee jumping...a dive into the river. It was five weeks of horror in and out of coma in a swirl of drug-induced delirium and tortuous medical intervention before he was set free and died. Oh, sorrow.

We are mortal and loved ones die and there is no solace for such sorrows, only the gauze of layered time to blunt the open truth of the wound. Michael left and his family is devastated. I don't need to say more of this, for it is the truth of life that death is universal and forever.

What I can tell you here is what I experienced following his death. It is that which I endeavor to convey. Regardless of lifelong search and determined avoidance of easy answers, what I realized, as I went to the portal of death with the soul of my nephew, is that whatever Conscious Deity that is the God of all being, is a Force of Love.

The Love of God: we are born of Love (the spark of life) and, in time, we return to Love. In the interim, our mortal lives are vital contributions to the mix of all things. It is what I know to be true.

"So, Michael," I said to the spirit of my nephew out there on the edge of mortality where the horizon is a rising curtain before a glow of sound and light and achingly beautiful emotion, "all the horror-show weeks in the hospital with the drugs and machines and errant fumbling surgery—can you be free of it?"

"Oh, you forget all that stuff, Uncle Bob," he said with grin and then, with sad final farewell to a beloved friend, I let go and he let go and he went back into the Love. Oh, joy.

So, you see, it isn't death that we need to fear.

And I did not hear the faltering of mortal energy vibrating from Arthur's violin. I heard in the vibrato perfection of emoted sound, in the sweep of reaching phrase, in the recital of an old man leaning into the curve of a grand piano—I heard the song of mortal moment transcended to timeless grace.

Well, that surely was worth the long drive, wasn't it?

And later, the next morning, I went to the old street where we had lived for years and I knocked on the door of Dan Calderon, the best neighbor in the history of human community. I saw him in there sitting on the couch probably watching *Oprah*, this eighty-year-old retired bricklayer/stone mason. He came to the door and in the hesitation of shock before we embraced, he said, "Robert, are you real?"

And in the parking lot of the senior-apartment complex, following a breakfast of toast, eggs, and whirlwinds of ideas and reflection upon literature, culture, and politics, I bade my dear friend and former teaching colleague, Jerry Stratton, farewell. I placed a hand upon his shoulder and told him I was aware he was getting his affairs in order and preparing to die. He said I was right. Jerry, once a priest, was still deeply Catholic. He was the most well-read person I'd ever known—an amazingly perceptive reader of my works. Jerry contemplated life with unrelenting religious and intellectual depth. And, in his mid-seventies, he was anticipating death. True to his beliefs, he had lived a life of mortal frailty in quest of Godly perfection and, thus, was ever fraught with blessing and guilt. So, I told him, out there on the parking lot where we knew our goodbyes could well be the last, about my nephew Michael and my moment on the edge of Ever. "You know me to be skeptical, perhaps even agnostic about matters of belief. You know I don't speak these words lightly. But, Jerry, I can tell you with a resounding certainty that God loves you and that the Love of God awaits you."

And then, his gift to me. The old pedagogue, the boom-voiced bellower of Shakespeare who made students quiver at the might of his impassioned recitations "Friends, Romans, countrymen, lend me your ears!"—my dear friend, wiped a tear from his eye and said, "Thank you, Robert."

Just when all this was getting too heavy, I spent a magical time with Lary and Sue Kleeman and their amazing five-year-old son, Niko. We sat out by a fire pit on their patio as night approached and ate popcorn to the dancing light and laughed as Niko painted me a picture, Sue spoke of health, and Lary relished it all. Lary is a fine poet. When I used to give guest talks to his classes, I would describe their teacher as the "second best poet I know personally." Of course, they would ask who was the best and I would feign modesty and say, "Well, that would be me."

Lary had a book for me. It was a beautifully bound and illustrated (by artist Sue) collection of his poems. I am mentioned among those listed in the dedication. Wow.

"How refreshing," I told them. "You guys are so alive."

(Most of this next story about Russell Hummel was included in my book, *about Mountain Living: Finding a Way*. It really belongs in this work too—in the context of the road trip where it happened.)

Near Grant, Colorado, I picked up Russell Hummel for breakfast as I headed back west toward home. I've written about Russell before. He was my high-mountain buddy, partner in toil and trouble, former boozing bud and forever co-conspirator in plots against normalcy. It was immediately obvious my brilliant and cantankerous old friend was really screwed up.

"Some kind of a little stroke, they tell me. I have a hard time...getting things said right.

"No, shit, Russell."

"Memory's not so good, either."

"Hey, in your case, maybe that's not such a bad idea."

What was I supposed to say? "Oh, Russell, I didn't know. I didn't notice the slur to your speech, the jerky pattern of your thought, the frustration in your eyes." No way. Once, after I had nearly lost a battle to some bodily assault and, after months of slow recuperation had finally returned to work, he had offered me the sensitive observation, "Cripes, Robert. You're weaker than a stick of hot butter."

So, he wasn't too surprised when I said, "You're kind of fucked up, aren't you, old friend."

"You could say that."

"You going to get better?" I asked.

"You're damned right, I am. They say it could take a year."

Russell was never known for his patience and those days he had to figure out how to give his own mind time to catch up with its own intentions. Damn!

We had eaten a meal at the Cutthroat Cafe in Bailey and were heading back up the canyon to where he and his dogs and cats live. I drove along the curving path of the South Platte River and he was pleasant enough because friends don't lay their sorrows on each other any more than they have to.

"You've done all right so far. What is it now, eighty years?"

"Damn near eighty-two."

"You'll get through this, won't you?"

I'll tell you about the time I told old Russell that I loved him. I was in a big hospital in Corvallis, Oregon. I had been flat out and nearly dead from blood poisoning of some nasty sort. They weren't promising Carol anything and, to tell the truth, I wasn't too sure about it either. But then, after intensive care for a couple of days, all those drugs they had been pumping through me started to take hold and, maybe I'd live after all. We were all pretty happy about it with life opening up again before us. Carol was there and Kristin and my sister Nancy and the nurses were good people and really cared about me. When death had a good grip on me, I didn't really feel much.

It wasn't until life came resurging back through all the tissues and fibers of my being that I really starting coming apart.

So, I called Russell back in Colorado. He's a gruff old piece of work. Foul mouthed and ornery on the outside, but a real sweetheart once you get past the piss and vinegar.

"Hey, Russell, they say I might live."

Carol had kept him up on my condition throughout the ordeal and he couldn't help but admit he was relieved. "Well, I'm mighty glad to hear that, Robert. Maybe you'll quit whining so much now. You've got no business putting Carol and Kristin through so much worry."

"I know. I sure hate to be a bother."

"Good. That's enough of this crap."

"But, Russell, I've got to tell you something." It sure was easy to cry during those delightful hours of hope and there were big hot tears coming down my face and I was probably sputtering a bit when I said, "I love you, Russell."

It was dead silent on the phone for a long pause and then I heard him clear his throat and he said, "Well, I love you, too, Robert. Now, do we ever have to do this again?"

"No."

"I sure hope not."

We usually babbled like mad men, shouting and laughing and telling all we knew about life and politics and spiritual wonders in a general and unrelenting rage against ignorance. But the miles were raging in silence as we both strove to say what couldn't be said.

"Damn it," he said.

"Yeah," I said.

All those years up in the high country and every turn in the road should have had a story to tell.

"They say...this...will take some time. Damned doctors, what the...hell do they know anyhow?"

"Say, Russell," I said, just thinking of twenty years of odd jobs and beers at the Platte River Inn and of Becky, his dangerously hostile and beautiful little wife who had looked up from folding clothes a couple of years earlier and said, "Russ," and then fallen dead on the laundry room floor. So much

109

passed.   "Russ, do you know why I moved out of the mountains and then on out to the coast as far west of Colorado as I could get?"

"No. I never did figure that one out."

"For twenty years you did your damnedest to kill me and I thought I'd better get out before you succeeded."

"Kill you?"

"Yeah. That's what I said."

"Now...come on...you take a few minor accidents...too personally, my boy."

"Personally. I'd say it was up close and personal when you started an avalanche of blocked logs rolling down the side of a mountain right where I happened to be standing."

"Come, on. That was just to test...your reflexes."

"How about when I was sitting on the tailgate of your pickup truck and you slammed it into reverse and backed into a tree?"

"You shouldn't have been sitting around, anyway."

"And the time I was under your little Honda working on the dangling exhaust system."

"Yeah, my little 'peanut' car."

"Well, you decided you needed a beer or something, started it up and drove off. I know I left some of my precious few final hairs under the tire."

"It was so quiet, how was I to know you were taking a nap under my car?"

Something was happening. Something wonderful. We started laughing about all the times he had dropped heavy objects on my head, shot air-hammer nails across job sites to stick in the wall where I was working. We laughed about the way he kept lining up roof work for us knowing full well that I'm afraid of heights. We laughed harder and harder and the words and the stories started spilling out in a flow.

"And what about the dead horse, Russell?"

"What dead horse?"

"You know what I'm talking about. Old Patrick."

"Now, that wasn't my fault, Robert. It was just a minor misunderstanding."

"Minor, my ass. And, by the way. Did it ever occur to you who paid that vet $50 to shoot your horse? What was it, ten years ago. I'll tell you who paid him. Me. That's who."

"Well, thank you, Robert. I'll get you a check in the mail tomorrow."

Flowing. And, God, we were laughing so hard I almost had to pull the car over.

"So, there I was chaining up the hind legs of that old dead horse to drag him off for a proper rest where the forest animals could make a good use of his carcass, all grief stricken, not to mention broke from giving my last fifty dollars away and you shouted from behind the wheel of the Land Rover, 'Ready!' And I said, 'No!' and you, you old deaf bastard, you heard 'Go!' and off you went. I came within inches of being trampled to death by a dead horse."

God what fun it was driving up that highway with my dear old friend and laughing like that.

"And how about when you asked me to help with that electrical problem and lightning hit?"

"Come on, Robert. You can't blame me for the damned lightning."

"I'm not so sure about that. KA-BANG and it blew me all the way across the room."

"You've got to give God a little credit for trying to kill you."

I pulled into the drive and down through the aspen trees to his cabin by the river.

With tears in my eyes, I said, "So long, Russell."

I hadn't really stopped and with each encounter, each heart-felt connection along the way, a bit of me was expended. When I drove the twenty turning miles off U.S. 50 up to the little mountain town of Pitkin planning on spending an hour or two with Anne and Gordon Possein, I was beat. They are wonderful artists—he with a chainsaw and chisel and subtle touch of sand paper and nuanced breath upon wood, she with pencil and watercolor and any medium she picks up and infuses with the full force of her touch and truth. When I arrived, I was embraced and cajoled and serenaded by Gordon on his banjo. I tried to join in with his

111

backup Banjo #2 but didn't have the stamina to keep up. Their son Benson was there and added to my sense of welcome, Anne made me a magical sandwich, Gordon and I took a walk of a mile or so up the dirt road with the creek beside and the great mountains rising green and the air a-chill with twilight. Man, was I tired, but good mountains and the conversation with wonderful friends saved me from myself. They prevailed upon me to stay the night. I was babbling on about how amazing was the coincidence of finding good people at every stop of my journey— then I settled into a nest of pillows upon their large couch and didn't stir until breakfast.

It is a poem, you know.

A poem of art, and art was everywhere from the harsh truth of Wyoming to the gentle truth of a night's rest in the home of great friends.

I had dreaded calling Meezie Keyes. She was old and really dying—not just contemplating death like Jerry Stratton or staggering a bit with intimations of mortality like Arthur. Meezie was nearly ninety and had been dying of lung cancer for a couple of years at least. I kept in touch with e-mail communication about science and other funny stuff with her husband, Dick Stacy. He sent me articles about astronomy and chemistry and philosophy and I tried to come up with sensible responses. Of course, in the mix of galaxies and geezer jokes there was interspersed connections of the affection we three shared.

I dreaded calling because it is hard to call when you don't know what to expect. Meezie was an amazing woman, a college-educated, sophisticated, down-to-earth genuine cowgirl whose wit and lovely laughter had enchanted me for years. I didn't want to find her moribund or worse.

But call I did and she answered and, hallelujah, she was there and alive and as vibrant and engaging as ever. "Sure, Robert. You come and see me, but you'll have to give me a kiss," she said.

"It's about time I gave you a kiss. I'll be there tomorrow morning about eleven."

A half hour down to the highway from Pitkin, on west through Gunnison and then sixty miles to Montrose. I was there early and stopped at a local coffeehouse. It was a marvel to me how well

112

this sequence of profound encounters had been falling into place. I told you this journey was a poem—I think a sacred poem, actually. The night before I left Denver I went up to the casino town of Blackhawk with my old buddy Jerry Branting. Jerry is a retired music teacher, part-time musician, and professional gambler. That's right, he went from marching bands and concerts to mountain dens of electronic risk. We were enjoying a hundred-dollar steak dinner together—compliments of the establishment—and talking about something he had said to me a few months earlier. We had been talking about music and art in general. Jerry is an accomplished horn player and really knows his stuff. I told him of the difficulty I had experienced when trying to record the playing of a couple classical violinist friends. "They're never satisfied. It's got to be perfect with them."

Jerry thought about it for a moment. He's a delightfully laid-back sort who enjoys life with open enthusiasm and little sense of self-importance. He said, "You know, I think sometimes perfection is the biggest obstacle to art."

I repeated his incredible insight to him as we sat with the deluxe spread of tender steak and all before us and he replied, "Did I say that?"

The point is, maybe what my philosophical old friend said to me may well apply to the broader sense of art to which I allude. The poem of the journey, for example.

It's not so much the perfection of the experience as it is the depth and sincerity of it.

Dick met me at the door with a handshake and a hug. "Meezie," he shouted. "Wake up. Robert's here."

Yes, I know this road trip is getting a bit long, my friend. But, trust me, telling the serendipity of encounter and gift that materialized at each segment of the journey is critical to the last scanned line of this poem.

All I really did there for my half-hour visit in Montrose was sit on Meezie's bed with her and hold her hand and share gentle laughter, a touch of tears, and a sweet wrenching presence of affection. Then I kissed her goodbye, hugged old Dick and left.

So simple the event, a lifetime in the gathering.

Western Colorado, Grand Junction, a good lunch with forty-year friends, Bob and Judy, and their amazingly furry and energetic dog, Buddy, and...on home.

That's all.

Yes, if in fact Ms. Lee was right and this is "*all there is*," it's a good thing. "All there is" it is almost more than my heart can bear.

Robert Nichols / Arthur Knebel
Friends: Mind and Spirit
2011

The Songs We Sing

With mumbled groan, we sing along with the songs blaring from earbud headphones and drive nuts the excluded audience of the rest of the world within earshot of our slurring glee. Sometimes it's even worse with me. I not only mumble/join the melodies spilling forth from the tiny electronic library in my shirt pocket, I often am inclined to leap into impromptu dance. I can't help myself. It's the music.

We love to sing, we love to join in, we love the motion and emotion of the tune, the rhythm, the expression of music. It's as natural as words themselves. Some say song may have been the first touch of communal messaging in early humanoids. First the inarticulate murmurings of song; later the *Oxford English Dictionary*.

Once, it was at the funeral of Russell Hummel's mother, Carol and I were standing with the congregated mourners at a really holy, fundamentalist church where they were sending her off to Jesus and about to commence singing a wonderful old hymn. That day I had a terrible case of some kind of throat misery that gave me the voice of a bass ogre in a choir from hell. Carol jabbed me in the ribs and whispered that she would give me twenty dollars if I wouldn't sing. Twenty buckaroos, man that was a lot of wealth for me to consider—and just for a few minutes of silence. "Okay," I thought to myself. "I can do this. I can avoid further injury to my voice, avoid embarrassment to my dear wife, and make twenty bucks to boot. I can do this," I thought as the verse flowed dangerously close to the chorus. And then, in an uncontrollable growl of rasping fervor, I could stand it no longer, and cut loose, full throttle with a voice that nearly rattled the lead right out of the stained glass windows. "Then sings my soul, my Savior God, to thee..."

I couldn't help myself.

Another old hymn says it best, "How can I keep from singing."

115

In our modern world, music is everywhere. Gooey tunes have spread from the elevators like mold, evolved into more assertive modes of expression, and now inhabit most every quarter of our ambience—from grocery stores to doctor's offices to restaurants—incessantly in the background of our conscious existence. Miniature electro-marvels broadcast from our pockets to tiny speakers in our ears. The radio plays on forever and the songs never stop.

On and on and, regardless of intensity or sophistication, we spend our whole lives in a little box where elevator music is forever.

"Hey, dude" you say. "My tunes ain't no elevator music. It's gansta rap, hip hop mean, Pink Floyd funky, Vivaldi vibrant, country true, and heavy, man, heavy. Do you dig?"

Well okay. Sorry if I offended your delicate artistic sensitivities, but my point is, whatever the character of the tunes you play, they are everywhere. And, as such, though by familiarity seemingly innocuous, they are deeply significant in the enactment of your days.

Years ago, back in the early seventies, I did a little experiment with my 9th-grade English students at Grand Junction Junior High. I challenged them to tell me the meaning of the words to the songs they were playing on their home stereos and demanding of the DJ's at after-school dances. This was at the tumultuous time when hippy love music was being supplanted in the nation's psyche with 'heavy metal' ditties. I read the lyrics to a particularly odious work by a popular group and asked my students what they meant. "It's the beat, Mr. Nichols. We just love the beat."

"Well, yes, there is plenty of beat here but do you realize this song is encouraging a suicidal dive into the black waters of the wells of Hell?"

"It's the beat, Mr. Nichols. We just love the beat."

I love the beat, too. With me, it's not so much the machine-gun rhythms predominant in most of the recordings produced for the past half century as it is the primal beat of an Indian or Himalayan chant, the heartbeat driving power of deep drums, the truth of an Irish jig. Whatever it takes to stir the basis of human emotion deep within the fibers of the collective memory of our tissues. I mean, sometimes you've just got to dance.

But, I'll tell you what. It's not just the beat. Our amazing complex of sense and mind absorbs all manner of emanation within range. If you think that some screaming fool, howling misery and discontent to the toe-tapping thunder of a three-story stack of speakers is just a matter of rhythmic thump and garbled verbiage, think again. The question must be: Does the ubiquitous mumble of music that infests the span of your day give lift to the mortal burdens you bear, or does it just pile the sorrows and aggravations heavier and heavier upon your being?

Is there the allure of a black well of Hell before you, or is there a blue bird on your shoulder?

So, what's on your iPod?

Zip-a-dee-doo-dah,
Zip-a-dee-ay.
My, oh my,
what a wonderful day...

117

Dimensions

The measure of ever?

Lady curves?

Man sized?

Navigation to 'where we're at, Dude?'

Dimensions...with three of them we live in *The House of Wax* (a late '50s 3-D movie I wasn't allowed to see).

Add the fourth (time) and we become mortal.

Add another seven and, call me a Bohr, we're talking physics. (When I studied physics in high school it was so basic we spent the first semester discussing Milk of Magnesia and Ex-Lax.)

Take them all away and we need to consult the Buddha to determine if we are nowhere or everywhere.

Okay. No answers here. I'm not the answer man. Dimensions are critical to rug salesmen and 'string theory' apologists but none of us should ever take them for granted. I have a story about a man who escapes from Evil by hiding in a micro-world of two dimensions. The bad guys searched everywhere for our hero but with no luck. He was right there on the shelf living with the family of a kind farmer, on a sheet of paper stuck in a copy of an old book. (You've heard of this family—he had a cousin who played bluegrass with Earl Skruggs. Get it? Lester Flatt—the Flat family...two dimensions. Come on, Dear Reader, this is some deep stuff but never serious. Jeez-o, peez-o. You probably didn't get the one about Niels Bohr, the famous physicist, or high school physics, as in a laxative like Milk of Magnesia either. I'm on a roll here, lighten up.) He was happy with the nice people but really missed depth. He would play games with the little kids (they could play tag but, of course, when they tossed a football around, he could never tell them to go out deep for a pass). He respected the farmer and helped him with his chores but they didn't raise many crops. Nobody ever got hungry because stomachs never sunk empty or swelled full. The farmer's lovely wife had a hot sister and

119

the man really wanted to hug her, but, you know, they could only nudge and tickle each other. The man wondered how the flat people mated, but was too polite to ask.

You get the idea. And don't worry about the man in the story. The family knew he had a secret and eventually they poked and cajoled and teased the truth out of him and they all went full-sized and 3-D and became dairy farmers. By time the bad guys came back around, he and his wife (the hot sister-in-law really filled out nicely) and their little pair of buttercup babies were all so round and jolly Evil didn't recognize the man and passed right on by him.

What's important here is not that we establish precise definitions of dimension. What we need to do is realize our primitive senses are only picking up the most basic emanations of reality. What we measure in three or four or even eleven dimensions is only a minute inkling of the vast and wondrous 'stuff' of all. Just think of it. Loving it up in three dimensions is a kick. Imagine another score or so angles added to an embrace. Wow.

It's true.

"And how," you inquire, "do you, a petty poet—a mere Bob in a world of Dylans, Bjorns, and Tyler-Taylor-Jeremiahs—claim to know so much more than height, width, depth, and 'hey, Bub, ya the time?'"

Well, the fact is, my buddy Dead Jack and his cousin God told me.

"God told you?"

Yeah. Well, not God like Zeus or Jehovah. More like a local deity who likes to call Himself Omni, as in *omni*present.

"A God talks to you?"

Sure. What? He doesn't talk to you? Oh...well, anyway, Omni says it's all like colors and rainbows, you know, the spectrum of visible light and... wait, why don't I just have Omni tell you Himself.

He's here now. Always is.

You've got that right, My Friend!

So, would you give our reader a run down on how things really are?

Okay.

I could speak in roaring wind and rushing water but you wouldn't understand. I could tell, with night-sky clarity, in galaxy and moon-chill, the essence of your most careful and secreted heart. With the stroke of a joke I could crumble your walls. With a whisper of unveiled wonder I could make mute any boast you've ever spoken of knowing.

But, take me seriously and you're not only misguided, you're likely miserable most of the time, too. Sorry, but that's the truth. Take earthquakes and epidemics and big hairy spiders seriously, but never a God. We didn't create this garden of a Universe, this nurturing planet, this precious home where you dwell and evolve for the sake of some holy hogwash of a jealous god ego-fest. What a crock. Mortals, it's supposed to be a party. I don't mean some drunken brawl drink-'til-you-barf orgy of epicurean excess (not that an occasional blowout isn't fun); but a party in the sense of an ongoing celebration of life. A party like getting together and singing hearts out about how much you love Jesus instead of how much you hate heathens; or, in summer night moon-shadows, dancing among Earth Goddesses until fertile urges rage hot and insistent for embrace; or like on some early spring mountain morning with snow yet fresh in the highlands and the day still a promise of poetry, when, with steam rising, you sip a good cup of coffee and smile.

Get it? A celebration.

So you want me to tell our reader about dimensions. Sure. But let's get something straight from the start. We're talking about matters no human will ever grasp. Colors beyond *Homo sapiens'* eyes, sounds beyond the 88 keys of the grandest Steinway. Love that would literally melt a human heart with intensity. (Taken beyond metaphor, it's not a pretty sight.)

Whether you be physicist, priest, or even some old roadside hippy, you won't get this.

But, by God, how vital it is to your purpose in this grand scheme that you marvel daily at the enigma.

Many religions speak of 'The Mystery' with authority, as if the imponderable reach of being were simply a secret kept by

121

their over-priced priests. To any self-anointed prophets of certainty I query, "What is the span of love's reach, the girth of God's heart? Which of your measures can quantify the mass, the weight of sorrow? You know, how many angels can you fit into a VW bug?"

See. By count of all man's known dimensions, by tally of all senses, by the cognizance and interpretation of all the grasp of your art and mind, the simplest touch of dew drops upon the sunrise-glistening leaves of morning bespeak poetry, song and science beyond utterance.

I do not boast—but, frankly, people, it's time to get over yourselves and quit peddling medieval fairy tales as astrophysics. Surprise, not only is Earth not the center of the Universe; the Universe isn't even a big deal in the hilarity of Ever. Universes are as common as flies at a feedlot. And you, humanity—created in God's image. Yeah, sure. The creative essence that sweeps stardust galaxies into wildflower meadows, cardiovascular networks and birdsong mornings, looks just like your Uncle Melvin or Aunt Gurtie? Hey, if you really want to know what even a minor God looks like, imagine the grandest sunset over the curling quintessence of the wildest turning dance of the sea. Then realize you're getting but a glimpse, a poetic suggestion of a half-second's essence of a hinder pimple on the passing ass of a sub-deity. I'm not saying I'm pretty, but do you really think a God would have anything as inefficient and leaky as a nose? Do you think Gods dine on Ambrosia and then, with the gastrointestinal configuration of a human animal, step out on the back porch of some Celestial Manse and blow farts? Well...maybe on occasion...but, you get the point.

Get humble or you're just wasting my time.

Humble isn't all that bad, really. I'm humble. You might not think so after my little tirade on what a minuscule bit of ego and babble you are, but the truth is, I'm not all that much myself. I'm just a minor Observer of a minor Universe. Just a means of gathering sentient data and conveying it to the really Big Gods and Beyond. And, oh yes, one other matter. I'm a means of conveying Love and Compassion from the really Big Gods and Beyond to each of you sentient specks of

122

intellect and wonder. You—what you know and feel and experience—are a crucial element in an infinite continuity of awareness. So, don't feel too slighted by my listing of your limitations. It's only a matter of scale. The example I revealed to Robert in *God of the Poets* related to the memory technique used to recall the colors of the visible spectrum. Remember your old friend Roy G. Biv?

R   red
O   orange
Y   yellow

G   green

B   blue
I   indigo
V   violet

Now, imagine that friend Roy represents all the light waves you can see and, then, imagine a big fat metropolitan edition of a phone book just packed full of other 'ROY' mnemonic names recalling 'rainbows' you have insufficient sensory and/or cerebral prowess to perceive. See what I'm getting at here? Light is just the beginning, too. There are many emanations.

You cannot quantify this super reality. I don't care how many blackboards you use to mathematically express descriptors of the vastness in which you are so deeply, intimately embedded—forget your mega-assed computers, you're just slapping beads on an abacus. You don't get it.

Thank you, Omni. I think we get your point. It's like when I would visit my father. I was in my sixties and he thirty years older. We'd talk for hours and sometimes, just when I would think I had really starting to get my ideas and observations over to him, he'd give me one of his *looks* and say, "Robert, you don't know anything."

It must have been difficult for such a passionate poet as yourself to have spent all these decades gathering knowledge and wisdom with mind and heart, just to receive blanket dismissal from the one person whom you had sought to please your entire life.

Well, yeah. It was pretty harsh.

And the worst part of it...

...he was right. Wasn't he?

Now we're getting somewhere.

This is getting discouraging. So, what's left? I tried being a Maytag Man for a few years and it didn't seem to be my life's big calling. Truck driving was fun for a while. Teaching school was deep enough but leading young minds to literature and creative expression just intensified my obsession to write my own literature. I'm a decent carpenter but I keep pounding my left thumb into a coaster—handy for patio parties but rather painful. I don't really have a choice, Omni. You know this. I'm a writer. If I don't write, I'll wither.

And...

And all you're telling me is no matter how evolved my craft may be, no matter how poetic the prose, artful the exposition, rich the texture, the reach, the flow of the language—I really don't have anything worth saying.

It would seem that way, wouldn't it?

Thanks, Dad.

Truth, my friend. Just truth. Look, as long as you measure yourself by the standards of certified public accountants, research scientists, and Sunday school teachers you, truly, have nothing to say.

What now, God? What am I to do?

Ease up, Poetman. I'm not here to shut down the art. I'm here to tell you why you are a poet. But the first thing you have to do is quit thinking so much and let yourself feel this world you crave to know. Feel it!

Robert, just be a poet.

Every aspect of the Universe of which you humans are aware is subjectively projected to your consciousness by the incomplete imagery of the mind. The only reality you know is what your mind interprets from raw sensory data. The rational universe (just God's big damn clock, *tick tock/tick tock*) is purely a construct of the rational mind's projection of insufficient data. Children and mystics have so much more fun than such analytical thinkers. They have so many more toys to play with.

Here's an example. Think about the best meal you ever cooked—maybe a big pot of chili that really hit the spot. A good scientist could replicate that chili over and over and it would never vary from a perfect blend of beans and spices—gallons and gallons of your concocted medley manifesting ideal texture and temperature. No problem for a good chemist. Right?

Wrong. With each steaming bowl served about the table, with each blissfully finite spoonful of the shared feast, with each heartfelt nod of appreciation—you and your beloved friends were enacting a shared experience never in existence to be known again.

Think about the subjective nature of such a pure and singular encounter. For a meal to be savored there must be an intersection of flavorful food with hearty appetite. For a feast to be successful there must be a mutually shared sense of celebration among enthusiastic participants. This great meal of yours was not just an occasion of the ingestion of a quantitative combination of onions and cumin and cayenne and secret powders and salts. It was the one instance in all the eon-sprawl of time that a particular group of the right

125

people gathered around the right pot of beans and, with each spoonful, partook of the essence of eternity.

Such is the nature of each day—subjective, irreducible, and unique.

So...I don't know anything but I have the potential for cooking some damn fine chili. Right?

Yes.

And each day, a new meal to be created from experience and shared.

I knew a poet could handle a metaphor.

So, where are we going with all this? Should I wake up our reader?

This might be a good time.

Okay. Hey, My Friend, sorry to stir your slumber, but I think Omni and I are about to conclude our dialogue and get on to the Big Guy's message.

Right. Here's the point and it's the reason you humans need poets and all other array of artists who, though baffled, are seldom silenced in their efforts to express the unspeakable. While you are incapable of measuring this vastness, you are fully capable of feeling far more than you are even remotely able to understand.
The most sophisticated apparatus you humans possess is more akin to what you derisively refer to as emotion. The Buddhists surmise it isn't what you say when you pray that matters; it's what you feel. Believe me, they're on to something.

Amen, Big Guy.

Anytime, Little Guy. Say, think you can handle this without me for a while? It's Ambrosia time on Cloud Nine. They're having fried chicken and I don't want to miss it.

Fried Chicken for the Gods?

Why not? Robert, do you remember your mother's fried chicken?

Remember it? Oh, yes, I recall. So dear the memory I could weep. God, yes, my mother's fried chicken. Something in the batter, a touch of seasoning, a touch of blessing. A family's soul gathered about those mother-loved Sunday meals. You're breaking my heart here, Omni. It's been decades now. She's been gone for over twenty years and, the last few years she was alive, Dad discouraged her from deep frying anything. She kept catching the kitchen on fire, bless her heart.

The Gods will be eating your mother's fried chicken today, Bobby Lee.

No kidding... I had no idea. Thanks, Omni. I...I didn't know.

Sure, my friend. Truth can be kind. And, tell me, right now with wet eyes and a heart of ache and love and sweet-sad sentiment, are your dimensions measurable by pounds and inches or real estate holdings or the net worth of your bank accounts; or are you, at best, described by a beautiful and futile poem striving to say the unsayable?

So, in a sweep, you take me from the impossible dimensional complexity of a physical reality, a Universe vastly beyond any glimpse of human comprehension, to an encounter with thought, sentiment, intimate closeness as personal and ego-finite as humans can know.

True.

I'm dizzy, God-friend. Swirling.

127

Wonderful, isn't it?

Yes. Of course it's wonderful. Almost more than I can handle.

Excellent! A precise balance between being overwhelmed by the immensity of human limitation, and being overwhelmed by the depths of emotions you are so richly capable of experiencing.

Mom's fried chicken. Just a little salt and pepper and a lot of love.

No *Secret recipe of eleven herbs and spices*?

Not hardly. Just hot oil in a skillet and a dash of simple 'this' and basic 'that' and, of course, a song in her heart as she danced about her kitchen. It's all emotions now, isn't it?

All. That's *all* it ever was. Or, actually, *is*. Yes, Robert, she does cook some fine chicken and I'm going to dinner now.

Bon appétit, Omni.

See?
Okay. The big *message* here is: Emotions are not reactive asides to the main dialogue. Emotions aren't the erratic babble of some sniveler's nervous condition. Emotions are not about whimpering and weeping.
Emotions are not amorphous, cloud-thin and irrelevant charge-lets of psycho-pap.
The myth of fact cloaks the fear of those who fail to touch their own hearts and know the fullness of living existence.
Feel it?
Emotions tell dimensions of reality far beyond even the imagination of the best of us. Emotions are the measure, the reality, the poem-bundle and bouquet of who we are.

128

Questions: Momentum of the Soul?

Let me stir up some questions. If you have ever pondered within your mind, or out loud with primal scream: WHY!!!?, this may help. Well, probably not, but who's going to fault the old poet for trying. You see, I have lived over 70 years, of which 55 have been devoutly dedicated to the art of saying, of communicating. And, not to brag, I'm pretty good at it, writing, that is. I can get it down with artful clarity, a touch of humor, honest expression of honest ideas. Yes, I'm a decent word guy, but also, I am a believer and practitioner of the sacred art/craft of Communication. It's a big deal with me, and by all the sacred, shouting whispers of my soul, I can't begin to tell you *WHY.'*

So, like so many of us for whom rote ritual and fairytale have proven useless in quest of Answers, even in the heat of wonder and the depths of awareness, joy has been obstructed by soul-edged frustration over the purpose of all this striving and loving and singing and weeping. I love that the world is more mystery than truth. I'm not talking about the mere tease and taunt of daily imponderables and cosmic cajolery. What I'm getting at is the reason some of us expend finite existence in wonder instead of just putting in our 40 hours/week and then sitting around drinking beer and talking huntin' and fishin' and football with our buds, or sipping wine and pondering fashion and diet and cosmetic surgery with our buddesses. "What's on the TV?" rather than "What's in the swirl of million-starred galaxies and the hum-song of Aeolian spider webs?"

I've heard people discuss football trivia as if they were debating the soul of Job.

Interesting, perhaps, but not of sufficient substance to qualify for space in this essay. In order to get to the angst-knotted heart of this, we need to approach sublimely impractical matters—you know, the stuff of angel-dancing on pin heads and astrophysical, dark-matter ghosties.

Let me propose mind-matters of greater gravity: Questions about the actual depth (or lack thereof) of human social intercourse.

We'll start with lips and then move on to robot love.

Then, once sufficient cerebral speculation has been aroused, once we're engulfed in impossible dilemmas, I'll move on to the final purpose of this section: enigma as *raison d'être*.

I was working on my relief carving, *Man/God; Sun and Moon*. It's a large cedar panel with an image of a primitive man clasping the crescent moon in his left arm and holding a blazing sun above his head with his up-stretched right arm. I was carving away on the muscular arms and the toes of the bare feet and the crazy-wild rays of the sun—just piling up the chips and sawdust, when it came time to do the fine work on the face.

Notebook sketch for *Man/God* carving
Robert Nichols / 2005

I like to start with the tear wells on each side of the top of the nose. The entire face can be pinned to these points, straight across to the eye balls sheltered by the brow, down the slope and over to the nostrils, and then on down to the mouth and its message. There is always great tension at this stage of a work. I am not such a craftsman that I can approach the significance of a face with nonchalance. There is always considerable risk when I start hollowing levels of recognition and expression from the flat plane of the wood. I start with the hard work of crafting a panel from 2 x 6 cedar planks. First comes the struggle for me, as a crude sketcher (take a good look at the drawing from which this work originated—it ain't DaVinci), to extrapolate from a spirit vision an image drawn upon rough wood. And then, carving in relief the shoulders, arms, digits, physique—approximating human form and all in preparation for the emergence of the delicate truth of the human face. Such an investment of time, art, and finite energy all at risk of ruin in the fashioning of the face. Scary business.

So, after procrastinating for an appropriate time, I fired up a carving tool and went to work. The God/Man reaches for the heavens, cradles the moon, and stands upon soil. His expression was to be one of weighty benevolence as he looked down from an elevation. He was to be, as a God, infused with the infinite; yet, as a man, accessible by mortal truth. "Wow! How are you going to do this, R-man?" I wondered. Yes, I wondered and carved, and wondered and after some vast and indeterminate stretch of time, God/Man really started coming alive for me. His eyes were giving; the contours, flaws, and lines of his face were telling of sacred journey and holy earthbound trial; the quest for universal harmony was emerging. Then, as I began forming the lips, I learned lessons in nuance that have marveled and perplexed me ever since.

It happened when I really screwed up the carving.

You see, it turns out that we perceive even the smallest alteration of the line, the fullness, the musculature of the mouth. I knew this in theory and in practice as a living breathing participant in non-verbal communication: as an active smiler and frowner. But, it wasn't until I started putting the final touches on the lips of what was approximating the face I had envisioned that I realized

131

just how attuned our awareness must be to minute shades of nuance in the everyday life of a smile.

My Man-God looked down from a slight elevation so his face needed to be slightly tilted forward. I stood back and, man-oh-man, there he was—his eyes just so and his time-sculpted flesh alive with contours of experience and his lips almost serious but not stern. Well...maybe a touch too stern. So, with my finest tools at hand, I attempted to 'lighten' the expression of my mythic man. Just a brush with pointed tip, a touch with a knife, a scrape with fine sand paper and, *voilà*, he went from slightly harsh...to outright goofy. No kidding. I mean, I'm a careful guy on this level—especially considering that most of my success with this art form I tend to attribute to the happenstance of chisel and wood grain and pure luck. I swear, I hardly touched the thing and, yet, there he was just some grinning clown of a character in a muscle suit.

Easily wrecked; easily restored, right?

Wrong. Every time I attempted to make a correction, I came up with different attitudes—arrogance, fear, disdain. From giddy grins to gritty threats, it was fascinating and frustrating. The amazing subtlety of facial expression was wonderful to realize. No wonder our brains are so much larger than they need to be to operate our bodies, write poetry, and launch rockets to the moon. Sure, it was fascinating, amazing, and wonderful; but, it was also eating away at the wood and, still, he didn't look right. I stood back and, then, in utter panic, I felt sick. I had carved his face so deeply that, rather than bestowing a look of compassionate blessing upon us mortals, my demigod had turned from outward emanation to inward naval contemplation.

Ruined.

Well...not really. We're talking wood here, not marble. Rough wood, at that. Once I overcame my initial despair, I went to work with a saw and cut the whole head right out of the panel and replaced it with a square of new wood and started over. Within a couple of hours, he had a new face and, to my delight, I hit the mark on the mouth almost right off. I can't begin to tell you what the difference is. I'm a word man and nuance and subtlety are the tools of my trade but I'm talking degrees that defy words. Sure, when you look at this work, after initial encounter with the overall image, you can see the lines where I glued in the repair piece but I think it adds to the overall charm of the big guy.

Okay, lips are amazing transmitters of attitude and emotion; eyes and brains are amazing receptors of subtleties of non-verbal expression. It makes you wonder about all of our senses, doesn't it? You know, from six meanings of the Chinese word *ma* when spoken at different pitches, to pheromone love-fragrances, to heated discussions of the merits and failures of a Mexican restaurant—our nift-o five senses are a marvel. Just makes you want to go right out and perceive, to sniff and stare and crane to hear; to taste the world and caress the textures of being with your incredible organs of awareness. Wow!

Now, just as we begin to bask in the vast prowess of our super-duper brains, let me raise some questions about the depth and sophistication of this sensory complex we call the modern human. Let's discuss robot love.

134

A while back I happened upon a report that described an experiment done by a scientist named Joseph Weisenbaum. In 1966, he designed a computer program that simulated the patient/analyst communication of Rogerian psychotherapy—a series of patient-initiated statements rephrased and echoed by the psychologist as questions.

This 'robot,' named ELIZA, was capable of simulating the same kind of interrogative semantic reactions as Carl Rogers had used to develop a psychoanalytic approach based upon the active personal relationship between doctor and patient rather than probing into the ancient history of the psyche in the style of Freud. This example I found on Wikipedia indicates what the computer was able to do.

Human: Well, my boyfriend made me come here.

ELIZA: Your boyfriend made you come here?

Human: He says I'm depressed much of the time.

ELIZA: I am sorry to hear you are depressed.

Human: It's true. I'm unhappy.

ELIZA: Do you think coming here will help you not to be depressed?

The result of this experiment, the ELIZA Effect, caused me to question the depth of all human communication. Even when patients knew they were being comforted and encouraged by a machine, they experienced positive effects from the interchange—a real sense of intimacy with wires and diodes and Dr. HAL.

Now, just a few thoughts. This is all about intellectual and spiritual curiosity: the depths we go to in quest of Cosmic conundrum and everyday paradox.

Are we humans the sophisticated, higher-functioning whiz-kid intellectuals we think we are, out here at the apex of evolution—

experiencing levels of love and warm fuzziness and spiritual enlightenment beyond the reckoning of all other sentient beings upon the planet? Or, are we humans but big, thin-skinned sacks of bio-parts just like bunnies and frogs and monkeys hopping and leaping and swinging about in quest of the stuff of biological biography: food, sex, and death?

Perhaps our famous "big brains" are autonomous entities, creating facades of pseudo-complex human reality, while maintaining a separate agenda. Massive nets of neuron goo humming and whirring and doing god-knows-what work in dimensions beyond the gloss of frappe societies and revved-up particle accelerators.

Perhaps complex 'relationships' are just brain teasers to keep us from becoming bored with the mundane reality of our corporeal existences (eat, screw, die, right?).

And, this hidden super-brain, could it be a function—a sensate source of data, processed and synthesized—of the ever-mysterious, elusive essence we call the 'mind?'

Do robots trivialize a complex and sublime system of verbal and non-verbal communication or, in fact, are we humans as shallow as the ELIZA Effect would indicate? Shallow as robotic compassion?

Do we humanize our pets, or are all communications primal—only given pseudo-sophistication by facades of complexity masking the truth of guts and loins? Are all communications as primal as the wag of a dog's tail?

Remember the joke about the dog who thinks his name is "get the hell off the couch."

Male sexual communication: Hallmark cliché, personal poem, or a complex system of rationalizing a basic tits-and-ass reaction to the female form?

Do we interact with sentient beings with depth or mere rote gestures of stimulus-response? Is this thing we call love a matter of poetry or just the salivation of crude biology?

And how do we reconcile the incredible sophistication of our subtle awareness of facial nuance with the crudity of robot love? Maybe that's the secret. If it's all as shallow as a smile, then we'd better be good at analyzing smiles, right? I mean, talk about pair-bonding ducks. Just how do ducks tell one mallard from the next? To me, they all look exactly alike. All the males have lovely, iridescent feathers arrayed in the same pattern; all the females are pretty much dull brown (camouflage) with secret little under-wing patches of color. Seen one, seen them all, true? Well, tell that to the lady duck I saw just mumbling about, nibbling at bugs, when her mate started doing the duck-ly deed with some floozy across the pond. She went wild. With a quacking scream she leaped into action and chased the slut out of the pond and clear out of the sky. If ducks are so discerning of physical identity, then why not we humans?

It makes you wonder, doesn't it?

And, of course, the only important question here: Who gives a hoot, (or a quack) anyway?

I don't have answers for the questions I pose—just a brainstorm of intellectual blather. What difference does it make if our amorous inclinations are more akin to puppy leg-love than the passions of a Shakespearean sonnet? Regardless of such speculation, today will spin on into darkness and the mortgage payment goes on and mortal moments click away forever. Why waste time with brain games when our reality couldn't give a flying flip at the moon about such contemplation?

Now, here's a thought. Maybe it isn't the basic biological, instinctual action/reaction, diddle-and-eat, pleasure/pain existence that finally defines us. True, we are likely just hump-and-slumber ape-oids at the level of functional reality. But, I think there's more to it than a robot or a dog or even a tabloid movie star can illicit.

Sometimes when I was a kid sitting at the kitchen table doing my homework—no, more likely sitting there reading a comic book, my mom would just kind of walk by and stop to scratch my head for a moment. I would feel like I had a place in the Universe when she did that. Maybe that's the key to this. I doubt if my big dog Jesse thinks about the Universe when I give him his good morning head massage.

Jesse and Robert contemplating the day.

Perhaps the most human thing we do is wonder.

A Summary Observation on
the Purpose of Life: Frustration With *WHY*

Answer: The question *Why* is not only the energy that drives mortal existence; the 'question' is also *the answer.* We are mortal, alive, sentient, loved and loving in this universe *to wonder.* An open eye is a question: "What's out there?"
Wonder is energy, momentum.

The Quest for Universals: Art and Wonder

Art makes solitary beings of the best of us.

Art, as the refinement and expression of the unique perception of an individual, isolates the artist in personal revelation. And by art I mean the attempts that any of us make to tell or show, to express who we are to another. Art, by absolute definition, must communicate. And, here it is, art communicates by expressing the message by means that transcend the ego and connect to the greater world. The medium of such arcing verbal, auditory, visual synapse is the *Universal.* Start with our universal fascination with clouds and their storms, then remember baby fear, sing *You Are My Sunshine...*weep at a sentimental movie and you are not alone.

During the early eighties, I taught in an innovative program at a junior high school. I was part of a team of four teachers—Luann the math lady/team hottie, Dennis the science whiz, and Flo the social studies/conceptual coordinator (she was a creator of the program and, thus, received most of the hate mail—I didn't even know what a *damned secular humanist* was until I discovered I was one), and I was the poet, I mean, English teacher. Each morning we four met first period and planned the day of teaching each other's lessons. The idea was that through interdisciplinary instruction the needs of emerging adolescents (i.e. hormone-crazed 7th graders) could be better addressed—the whole student being the subject of our teaching, not just the junior mathematician/scientist/citizen/participle dangler. I loved it. Albeit, it was a real job and, thus, daunting of the creative spirit in its temporal restrictions. I had to show up every day at the same time and account for my actions. But, it was usually creatively and intellectually challenging, personally rewarding, and paid more than I had been making hosing down gore at a packing house. Not bad.

And the team was super. Flo kept me ever on my toes professionally and had a wonderful wit and wildness about her (she eventually got promoted and ran the school). Dennis was the genius who taught me to realign the desks in my classroom between classes ("At least start with order.") and told me "Every crazy little fucker in your class has at least one crazy parent." (Dennis quit the team and became an amazing special education teacher.) Luann, well, what can I say. She was really sexy and sweet and loved to use the word Platonic around horny me. (She went back to school and got a degree in electrical engineering.)

So there we were each school day morning, gathered about a table in some cubbyhole of a conference room racing through plans and approaches and sharing our diverse views of students in need and firing up another round of education. It was called the HAIL program for Humanistic Approach to Interdisciplinary Learning. Of course, the majority of our rather conservative colleagues at the school considered us nuts-o, commie, Satan worshipers. But, hey, I'm a poet. I'm, ironically for a communicator, used to being misunderstood. Being neither beatnik (too young) nor hippie (too old) yet not the least bit mainstream in either attitude or appearance, this was just another foray into bastions of normalcy to kill a little time, pay a few bills, and appease societal expectations while awaiting the will of the Muses. No big deal that I was going to burn in hell for associating with secular humanists.

In an interesting and, likely, intended coincidence, a fellow from the traditional social studies department shared our planning time, and each day would situate himself in the corner of the conference room and say little. He was the arch-conservative of the faculty. More than any other member of the right-leaning teachers at the school, he probably thought we represented a menace to society. How he managed to remain a stoic observer of our raving rituals of passionate touchy-feely education was a wonder. He was a dignified looking gentleman in his forties— intelligent, scholarly, and, in my mind, absolutely head-up-the-hiney ignorant.

You know the type. They run the world.

We were cordial enough, but, throughout most of that first year of my inclusion on the team, he and I seemed to share no common ground of humanity upon which to converse beyond a mumbled, "Good morning (asshole)," from me, and a nodded, "Good morning, Bob (pinko, hippie, liberal swine)," from him.

And then one Monday morning in early spring everything changed. Everything.

By the happenstance of perfunctory small talk, we realized we had both taken our daughters to see an old Disney movie that weekend. I didn't even know such as he were even capable of the intimacy prerequisite to procreation, much less that he had a little girl whom he would take to a movie. It was wonderful. It turns out even fascist pigs and commie liberals can communicate on a real level if the right subject is breached. Something exciting happened. Something crumbled between us. It turned out in the giddy honesty of that encounter, both of us revealed that at some sappy, sentimental, Disney-deep moment in the movie, I think it was after a child was injured being thrown from a horse, we had sniffed back tears. This John Birch conservative and, me, a bleeding-heart liberal had known a near-sob sweep of emotion, not at a book burning or a flag burning but at a heart wrenching cine-magical moment of sweet sorrow.

I don't think we ever silently despised each other again.

If art, deep and meaningful human communication, is ever to actualize it must be in the realm of the *Universal*—a commonality of human experience that connects disparate paths.

Now, let's get down to the real stuff of our everyday prosaic existences. You know—work, kids, sports, beer, fashion and the eternal buzz and glow of ubiquitous media. Shallow matters generally, only made profound when jeopardized by health, or sexual or financial complications. It's about art. I always start with art because art represents the deepest, most individual parts of each of us, whether we spend our days painting church ceilings or painting picket fences. The deeper we go within ourselves as we distinguish our lives by our unique experiences and perceptions, the more we are alone and, thus, in need of the comfort of universal connections. We can start with mutual appreciation of the nurture of sunshine or the pleasure of a drink of cold water and we are never truly alone. It's why we talk about the weather so much. There's nothing trivial about such conversation. It's basic, it's real, and it is universal in its effect upon our lives.

So, perhaps it's time to revisit lips, robot love, and wonder. We may well be more amazing than we think. I mean, all of us. Even the dullest little pale fellow in the back corner of the accounting department; the plainest flower lost to the weeds of the untended garden of her life; the biggest cell phone shouting jerk in the coffee house—all humans have got to find means of soothing the ache of isolation integral to our artfully intellectual and biological selves. We need to touch, we need to find universal ground upon which to stand together and, as human beings, express our capacity, our need, our blood-soul-deep sense of wonder!

We are all:

1. **Subtle perceivers of nuance**—the facial, auditory, olfactory messages of the flesh.

In 1964, while traveling around the summer of my 19th year, at the Genesee County Fair in New York, a pretty young girl winked at me and I'm not over it yet. Sure, my traveling bud that summer, Walt Greenwood, claims she actually winked at him. Like hell she did, Walt. No matter, though. I never spoke to her. Too shy, too insecure of my charm, too afraid that she really had winked at Walt—who knows why it is that some moments are consumed by the energy of their creation. The memory of that complex of pretty lips, bright eyes and ocular tic is indelibly imprinted within me.

2. We are all: **Saps for the effects of a wagging tail or a cliché love poem.**

Years ago, up in the mountains at Al Gross' Platte River Inn, whenever the beer cooler kicked in the whole place vibrated. A buddy of mine, a hairy old mountain thing—he looked a lot like me back in those days—was sitting there having a Budweiser draft when the lovely girl who sat to his left said, "What's that shaking?" I mean she was only sitting beside him because it was the last stool at the bar. This guy had no expectations and a track record to back them up. But he went ahead and gave her a shot anyway. He looked right into her eyes and said with the best poem of his life, "I don't know. Looking at you, it might be the beating of my heart." Oh, the smile she gave him.

3. We are all: **Seekers of universals of connections**.

We bring a million different hearts and minds to *The Wall* in Washington, DC—this angling black slab of 58,272 deaths, this sable scar upon the soul of a nation, this singular focus of our million stories of war or defiance or confusion. This monument to sacrifice—nationally futile; personally sublime. I didn't go to war. I avoided the terrible decision to serve a cause I knew to be wrong or desert a nation I knew was better than the actions of its leaders. I dodged my generation's war by going to college, then going to teach, and finally drawing a draft lottery number in the high 280's (actually 288 in a year when 195 was the highest number called) and, thus, being removed from the list of the damned down at the Selective Service Office. (I suppose, to a certain degree, I escaped the conflict by being white and middle class and all but I sure wasn't complaining about injustice back then.) I didn't go. No shame; no sense of cowardice or dishonor; no regrets beyond an aching regret that the nation I loved had killed thousands upon thousands of Asians in their own homeland and over 50,000 of our young people upon foreign soil for outrageously stupid, arrogant, ignorant reasons. And, of course, sorrow for the good people whose lives were forever scarred by the horrors they witnessed; the horrors they perpetrated. So, what possible universal connection could an old draft dodger like me have with the time-ravaged, gray-haired vets who trace the names of their comrades etched into the wall and shamelessly, courageously weep for unfathomable loss? I'll tell you. Standing at the wall with sixty-year-old brothers, I share a common and devastatingly grave truth separate from the nightmare of those who did go. We stand together and together we hear the songs of the ebony wall—the long suffering song of the survivors; the tragic song of America's violent truths; the stone black song of the dead soldiers and, together, it breaks our hearts.

143

4. And, most of all, hallelujah, we are all: **Wonderers**.

"I wonder why Miss Quade's so mad at me."

"Jeezo-peezo, Peter. Didn't she just peel the paint off the room screaming that you were, 'insufferably impudent and rude?'"

It was 6th grade and out on the playground we were all still a bit stunned by our teacher's major tirade. Peter and a couple of his no-good buds (not me, of course) had wreaked havoc upon the learning process for much of the day before. And, with much justification, Miss Quade, in a raging Jekyll-to-Hyde metamorphosis, had rolled her old eyes back in her head and unleashed an amazing string of expletive-free but, nonetheless, damning descriptions of the agents of chaos who had invaded her careful and sacred classroom. I wasn't one of the perpetrators, but, still, it scared the hell out of me.

"Yeah, Nichols. But I wonder why she's so mad at me."

And, during the same year, I wondered if Julie Smith would be my first date and go with me to Lynn Benson's spring party—the first and only out-of-school party of my elementary school career. I loved the way Julie giggled at my jokes during free time and while toiling away at Miss Quade's terrible art projects (after spending months on creating papier-mâché puppets, my buddy Melvin and I, recalling history lessons about Joan of Arc, took ours home and burned them at the stake) and I loved how Julie smelled of some primal and mysterious pheromonal perfume when our eyes met and our elbows touched, and she had the cutest smile I had ever seen—you know, the first smile. I wondered, I dared to call, she said 'yes.' The date went terribly, the magic forever lost to awkwardness, and the moment of our love passed. I wondered, no, I still wonder what happened.

I wonder at the delightful happenstance of my haphazard life that brings me to this day of my loving wife Carol, my magical daughter Kristin, my unhindered access to creative opportunity. I wonder what the Gods have in store for me.

I wonder, now that the Higgs boson particle has popped out of the CERN super hadron collider if there is any better explanation of the resolution of *The Big Bang* into stardust and suns and planets and a 200-pound poet named me.

> And in the marvel
> of the inexplicable we call existence,
> we gather together upon hillsides
> with vistas
> of sunset horizons
> and endless seas,
> and of the night-sky sprawl and turn
> of a billion galaxies,
> and know the hilarity, the danger,
> the allure and fright of each other
> as together we wonder...
>
> Yes, together we wonder.

See? Do you understand now what I meant when I said, "The question is the answer?" You know, the question *WHY!* This is the *Universal* enhanced by perceptive nuance, biological challenge and excitation—the universal question that marks our uniqueness while sustaining our inclusion.

It is by this ubiquitous stirring of wonder at the mysteries and enigmas of our lives that we discover the common ground of passion that enables in us a sense of human connectedness.

Remember: curiosity may have killed the cat; wonder created the Buddha.

Man/God; Sun and Moon
Robert Nichols / 2005

Living in Your BIV

I call it "your Biv."

Recall our buddy and local god Omni and his image of a pile of phone-book sized listings of spectra? You go to one of them and look up the mnemonic name of the minute range of colors visible to human perception. Biv, Roy G.

Red Orange Yellow Green Blue Indigo Violet, Roy G. Biv, Earlier in this work, Omni, told us we don't even have a clue about the extent of Cosmic phenomena. And he tells us not to feel insignificant but, perhaps, a bit more humble in the assessment of our "two cents" worth about anything.

And, it's not just upon some celestial scale that we are limited. As a species we encounter a specific range of perception, but, also, as individuals, we experience the limitations of an individual 'BIV.' Each of us has our own range of perception. And I'm not just talking light waves here.

It can be as simple as shanties or mansions, row boats or yachts, a can of beans or platter of hand-massaged Kobe beef. Or living the life of a 17th Century Untouchable watching from squalor as they built the Taj Mahal. Or like 8th-grade math class and *love* is just one row over and doesn't even know you exist. Worlds exist beyond the reach of our limited spectra of vision or inclusion. Worlds of wonder or worlds of horror and misery. Colors so brilliant they would melt the mind, so harsh they would freeze the soul. Worlds of the Gods, the Rockefellers, the Hollywood headliners, the crack-house derelicts, the holy monks of compassion—worlds of all the *others* whom we are not.

You know, *rainbows* out of our range of perceptible frequency.

What shall we do?

Envy, jealousy, and resentment are all but distractions to the rich reality of our local BIV. It's the actress Angelina Jolie's wonderful lips filling up a 40-foot-wide movie screen. I'll never kiss those luscious lips. But I can kiss Carol's luscious and considerably smaller

147

lips just about any time I can get ahold of her. And, don't get me wrong: this isn't a compromise, it's just a better fit. It's in the range of my BIV.

I'll tell you about one afternoon in 1961. I was having a Cherry Coke at the soda fountain down at Woodbridge Drugs. Darcie was such a lovely and friendly girl. She was in my homeroom at Gar-Field High School. She laughed at my jokes and I listened to her complex love stories. Her boyfriend was a Marine stationed at Quantico. It wasn't as if she was giving me any more than passing attention, but I knew she had that job at the counter and she always seemed pleased when I would show up.

I didn't even know there was butcher knife back there. A great big ugly butcher knife. The big fellow just walked behind the counter, picked it up and, before I could do much more than get the straw out of my mouth, he had me by the head and the blade right against my throat. And then, in some kind of half joking, half terrible guttural military twang he explained that Darcie was his woman and he hoped I clearly understood the fact.

With the sharp edge of that knife up against my delicate flesh, I was afraid to even nod my assurance that I got his point—or even speak for fear that a whisper might vibrate enough to get my jugular opened up. Darcie was sort of laughing and pleading and saying things like, "Oh, this is just Bob. He's nothing. He's just a guy from school. He means nothing to me. Now please put down that knife, Johnny."

He let me go but held on to the knife. "So, you're nothing. Is that right, Bob?"

"Nothing. That's right, big guy. Hell, I'm probably not even here," I said as I sidled off the stool and made for the side door exit. "Yes sir, I'm sure about that. I'm long gone and gone for good." I said as I removed my spectrum of existence from the proximity of Sweet Darcie's spectrum of existence. I never cared for cherry cokes that much anyway.

And as for Carol. I had no clear idea that she would ever be within the vibratory reach of the more profound frequencies of my world. I was nuts about her from when I first met her in the 2nd grade out there on the playground where little girls spun on the monkey bars. She was part of my 'visual' comprehension but it wasn't until our late teens that I realized we shared emotional

148

'colors.' It's about love and up in the woods near my folk's house at the end of a visit with her best friend, my sister Nancy, we kissed and in a quantum shift I realized 'kid brother of school friend' status was only the beginning.

What I'm trying to get to here is that, though our range of perception is limited—on a universal scale, minuscule in fact—and, on the level of human and natural interaction upon this planet—diversely and arbitrarily limited—it's all we get in the present incarnation. It's our BIV. No more; no less.

So, I'd better tell you about snorkeling off the coast of the Honduran Island of Roatan. Forget metaphor. I make no allegory of analysis in this example. This the stuff of physics: human beings can only visually discern light within a range from red to violet with a nice array in between. In a piece about this trip, I wrote about snorkeling and what, once I overcame the distraction of near-drowning (whiskers and face masks make for a difficult seal), I saw beneath the clear waters of a Caribbean reef.

> We waved at the flippered friends we had met the previous day during the "Dolphin Encounter" included in our deal, and headed along a short sandy path to the west side of Bailey Island to where the coral grows in shallow waters alee of the northeast storms.
>
> It was beautiful there with the sand and the water and the lush green land of tropical hillsides to the south and the arcing reach of the ocean spread forever to the north. A near-perfect place to make transition from land to sea. *Near* perfect, I say—not perfect.
>
> The current, the big clumsy flippers we wore, the abrasive deceit of coral clumps upon the rock sandy bottom: so fragile, delicate, and painfully harsh—it wasn't easy to get into the swirl of the shallows and cast off for the depths.
>
> I helped Carol and Kristin clear the shore and float out to the deep clear water. I watched as my dear people, with faces down and yellow snorkels up, gently kicked the waters and sailed away.

Okay, I thought, here we go again—another round of splash, choke, gasp and then back to the shin-banging torment of the shore. Just like usual.

I'm such a good sport. I stumbled in, expecting the worst.

But, wonder of days, this was not to be. Somehow, once afloat beyond the shallows, my mask fit snugly over the mess of my moustache, my breathing tube abounded with gurgle-free air, and, suddenly, the angst of the struggle forgotten, I realized I was flying. Beneath me, the coral forest grew in intricate complexities of chamber and chasm, fan and stem. And, donned in display of brilliant color beyond all extremes of terrestrial spectra, fish in gentle patterns went about their fish business oblivious to either me or the marvel of their own magnificence. Like an eagle buoyed by currents of rising air, I soared the sky-water surface as below me unique dimensions of remarkable hue and motion and grace revealed to me the humbling wonder of worlds beyond my experience.

Carol, from somewhere out toward the afore mentioned arcing horizon (so much for her assurances of staying by her man), shrieked and shouted with joy and startled excitment, the delight of her nose-to-nose near collision with a high-speed passing dolphin. Eureka!

Kristin spotted a barracuda.

And, from darken depth of a felt-pure void, there rose beneath me a flight, a school of blue, exquisitely rich, and sedate fish in random array giving visual caress to my awe, turning as one into the sun-glow revelation of their vivid translucence, and, then, disappearing forever into mystery.

And, thus was the sea.

I speak of the limitations of the visual, auditory—all the sensory ranges of our overt awareness. You know, our micro-peek at the infinite. Now, accepting that we can't go to movies projected in living gamma waves, or listen in on super-high-frequency conversations between bats, the actual reach of reality accessible to our human range of perception is amazing. I wrote about how our capacity for emotional experience far outreaches the input of our basic senses. In the expanded context of emotional awareness, what emanations we can know are exponentially exploded by the impact they may have upon our consciousness. When I swam/flew upon the sea-sky down in Roatan, from the secret world of reef life, I experienced intensities of hue that changed my life. I felt colors of God's energy a-swirl upon the emotional matrix of my soul—and all expressed within the limitations of a human's rainbow.

Not bad, huh?

"...the humbling wonder of worlds beyond my experience"—not beyond my perception.

I never left the spectrum of my abilities—I just explored its farthest depths.

So, love with all your heart, laugh with all your joy, embrace the truth and textures of your being and know, on some deeply personal and intensely involved level, though each uniquely our own: all BIVs are created equal.

So, the truth of the day is: Make the best of the life you live.

Live in your BIV—you'll be a lot happier.

Crow: Souls Departed; Souls Redeemed

Oh, sorrow, it was black feathers crumpled by the roadside: Crow was dead.

Oh, sorrow, a phone call on a summer afternoon: my father was dead.

It hadn't been easy for any of us those days—those months after Dad died. It wasn't like full-out mourning with sobbing grief and shudders of sadness. My good old papa lived well past his 96th birthday and died in his sleep. He wasn't even sick. He just finished his crossword puzzle (well, almost—I found two words unsolved, left for the next morning), filled his water glass, and went to bed. There were no signs of the struggle and tumult of mortal conflict by his bedside. Good night, my father.

I should have been doing fine—more empty than anything else. I caught myself heading for the phone to give him a call a few times. And there were sweeps of sad chill and the catching of breath in realization of the finality of such separation from this man I had loved and leaned upon and, with rage and roiling laughter, fought and embraced all the days of my life. Profound loss; not unbearable grief.

The funeral had gone well, I thought. We sang him out with some fine old songs and sent his soul to goodness. I spoke of my father and of his life and we laughed and we wept by his coffin out there in the July morning heat at the Quantico National Cemetery. I gave it my all. It was an accumulated product of a life dedicated to words. At last, by the grave I could answer his questions, his doubts, his accusations about the purpose of my poetry. I spoke with an eloquence borne of decades of seeking and saying. I had honored my dad's life with the art of my own life. It seemed right, until back at the house when my sister Nancy came to me with an aching sense of betrayal. I had spoken of *my* father, while she sat there needing to hear *our* father. She felt left out and the truth of her condemnation of my words nearly destroyed me. She knew there was no malice in my heart for her, but, by the stabbing angst of her pain, from a moment's soaring sense of the worth of my life's art I was shattered by a sense of final failure. You see, poets or any artists create from the deepest sense of the word "I." It's all ego with our truths, but the measure of our art is the extent to which our small stories embrace the heartfelt fibers of the universal identity of all who know them. I spoke of my father but, by art, spoke of fathers loved, respected, and lost to all who heard me. It's the stuff of poetry when it works. For most who attended the ceremony I had succeeded beyond my most ardent intent. But, for Nancy, alas, there was no art that day, only neglect.

I sat alone, slumped in a chair while downstairs there was the polite chatter of mourners gathered to eat and laugh and remember a great old man they all would miss. I was in a state of ruin, nearly choked breathless and with no way to rise. I had, with the full force of my being, devastated my father's daughter on the day of his funeral. Intellectually I knew I had done no wrong but the dynamics of strained expectation and misunderstanding are inherent in the complex that is a family and the damage was done.

Then, a voice I had never heard within myself spoke up and said, "Forget it. You did your best and it was good. She'll be alright." I thought, "Okay," and headed on down to the food and family and even had the whole assemblage of friends and loved ones belt out a round of "Happy Birthday" to Nancy. Oh, the irony of days.

Three months passed and, more than the expected remnant wake of sorrows following a loss, something was deeply disturbed in my inner makeup. I wasn't feeling right. Actually, it was as if my entire emotional interaction with life was muted. Daunted were the marvelous excesses of joy and sorrow that dance wildly the soul of a poet—opened to the full spectrum of life. I didn't laugh so deeply as was the truth of mirth, I didn't weep the depths of the beautiful pain of mortal being. My wife Carol suffered the most from this lapse of joy. It's in the pictures taken during those days. I wasn't truly smiling. She was suddenly living with a stranger.

Something was wrong. I was back home from the burial and well into a quick finish of his matters. He left my sister Nancy and me a nice sum to evenly divide–we aren't 'fixed' but put in better

154

repair for our ensuing days. I should have been okay. I'm tough and can handle what life offers up. But I wasn't. It's not that I don't feel the brunt of reality. I'm a damned poet. I feel with all the openness my heart can bear. I have endeavored throughout my life to stand fully aware before the raging winds of sad-sweet sorrow and exhilarating joy. It's the way to the truth—emotional reality is the only true reality. The rest is dull illusion, shapes and motions of a shallow facade. When I'm really on, I openly laugh with raging storms and weep shamelessly at maudlin movies.

Carol and I bickered constantly. You say, "So what, Bub. You're married." I'll tell you what. Carol and I are not just linked at the license, we are bound by souls and know the melding bliss of daily laughter and embrace. We might occasionally hoot, scream, and rattle the windows with momentary rages when I'm really wrong about something; but, we don't succumb to the seeping angst of petty ire. I was constantly impatient, she was aggressively defensive, and we were both alternating apologies and attacks. We were miserable. You see, the normal Robert is a crazed old dude, outrageous of speech, and sometimes obnoxious of wit, but, not insensitive. Not unkind or demeaning of word or attitude. I honestly give people cause to admire themselves.

Carol was in the middle of one of her regular computer dilemmas and I stood behind her and attempted to talk her through a maze of menu choices. She sensed my impatience with her and felt stupid and mad and I felt like screaming. With a flick I dismissed her hand and took control of the mouse. Huddled over her, frantically clicking commands, I felt the shudder of her weeping.

Later, as we drove along on a Costco run 50 miles over to Salem, we found something to laugh about and with the easing of tensions I was able to tell her the terrible truth I had come to realize within myself. "I don't feel anything," I told her.

"Your father has died. Sometimes being numb is a way people handle sadness," she said, trying to fashion some kind of excuse for my attitude.

"I don't think that's all of it. I'm not just hiding my feelings; I really don't have any. At least I don't feel with the depth that I need to be me. I don't feel like myself anymore."

155

"You aren't yourself," she told me. "I don't really know who you are sometimes."

And then with a shiver that coursed my entire being, I realized who I was and was seized with a silent panic from which I had no imaginable escape. The impatience, the surface insensitivity, the dismissal of difficult personal matters, the cool self-assurance about my sister Nancy, "Forget it. You did your best and it was good. She'll be all right."

"Carol, the spirit of my father has taken over my being. I am Robert Nichols *Senior.*"

It had happened the day of the funeral in the upstairs den where I was taking a break from the gathering and feeling right about what I had done. As I told you, my weeping sister came into the room, clasped me in a wrenching hug and told me of the terrible pain I had unintentionally inflicted upon her.

What she laid upon me in her perception of neglect, was more than I could possibly handle in the vulnerable state of my mind the day of the funeral, the day of my most powerful poem, the day of my most profound failure. I had sent the soul of *my* papa on its blissful way and then was told that I had excluded my sister from the ceremony honoring *our* father. The revelation was devastating, I could hardly breathe, I felt the stopping of my art. And just then, returning from the *great journey*, Robert L. Nichols, Sr. had taken over Robert L. Nichols, Jr. and rescued me from falling into a terrible abyss... He never wasted time with concern for matters he could not change. The damage was done. "She'll be alright," he had said from within my heart.

"Carol, I've become my father."

And she said, with sad resignation in her voice, "I loved your father. He was a good man and generous and kind to us, but, I would never want to be married to him."

"Hell, he was my dad and I loved him and respected him but I sure don't want to be him. It's empty in here where poems used to roil and rage and sing."

So, we drove on and for the next week or so we tried to quiet the misery and live with a dangerous truce—short of honesty but civil enough to abide.

We were driving up the coast. It was late October and the clear cool sun shone through clouds upon a sea that had turned toward winter wild. The great storms were gathering somewhere toward the northern pole and the waves were a-stir with portent energies. Carol and I heading north from Newport where the highway is an asphalt whim superimposed upon eternity's unsettled processes upon the edge of a continent. A squall engulfed the moment of our passage with wind and drench and then rainbow. It should have been another of the singular moments that make up the essence of a lifetime. But my father's heart within me only noted the components of God's art, not the wonder.

The rest of this, a story of Crow, salvation, and the Grand Canyon and the redemption of a lost soul, is strange and impossible to explain. I can only tell what I swear to be true. I can only recount subtle and overt events and hope sincerity may allay incredulity. My only proof is the presence of an old poet here flowing words from a heart no longer be-stilled, banished by grief.

I'll tell you briefly about my relationship with Crow.

We all need help. Sure, we are smart and educated and self-assured in our discourse with this world. When my daughter was a tiny thing and she would fall down, I told her, "What do we do when we fall down, Kristin?" And, even as a small child she knew the answer. "We get back up." Yes!

You can have as soft a heart as Is known to humanity, but you've still got to be tough. You've got to be able to handle the rough stuff that comes with being brave enough to really live. True, there are times when we know the irrepressible rising of our tears, but... "What do we do when we cry, Kristin?" Sometimes we just have to wipe our eyes, blow our noses and keep going. Sure. But we all need some help. We give it to each other and call it love, friendship, compassion. We chat, tweet, text and e-whatever, but we are, in fact, really still quite alone. Help.

I know love. I know friendship. I even think the Gods are compassionate. And when I fall, I can usually get back up.

The most isolated I have been was during a five-year period when I lived in a tipi high up in the Colorado mountains. During the winter the closest human contact was miles away and there was no phone service, no electricity, no one but me. I usually was not lonely, just alone. There was a good mountain tavern six

157

miles down the hill, and love, though somewhat latent, yet embraced my soul from an hour's drive to the city. No ascetic, no hermit—just a poet/mystic seeking his own truth and hints of the powers of the Universe while existing with no rent and little income. While I went to the literal extreme of living weird in the wilds, to some extent, regardless of the proximity of handy folks and creature comfort, we all know something of a self-imposed sense of isolation. It's critical to self-actualization. There are times when we all need to escape the cultural grid and find solace in our own beings. Right?

But, we all need help.

When I lived in such utter solitude, my best friends up there were crows. "Ravens, fool. We're ravens!" they would caw. But a raven is just a blackbird on steroids. I speak of all the black birds that accompany me collectively as 'Crow.' I would caw back to them as they circled or sat upon the outcropping rocks, "Crow!."

It wasn't like I fed them or they tamed their mystery to the point of sitting on my outstretched forearm. No. We didn't insult one another to that extent. We just conversed in sounds and, mostly in silence. They watched me for some time before they accepted my presence on their mountain. And, eventually, I came to realize they had honored me with their concern. They had adopted me and with vigilance, humor, and magic looked out for me. Seldom did anyone ever approach my camp without a screeching escort of the big black watch-crows calling out to me with warning of intrusion. And when it was hard to get up and get the words or prayers or music moving, when bitter cold or fickle art entrapped me in the womb of my old Polar Guard sleeping bag too long into the morning, with jarring song and penetrating eyes burning down through the smoke hole right into my benumbed being, Crow gave the urging I needed.

And, thus, I have been blessed. Even now, far from the rigors and wonders of the high mountains, living in the sweetness of love and comfort, my old friend Crow is ever near, still watching, still cajoling.

So, driving up from Newport in the rain and in the funk of insensate sorrows and alienation that afternoon of an October day three months past the passing of my dad, when Carol muttered a saddened, "Oh," I was startled from daunting introspection. "It's Crow," she said.

I bless all road-killed beasts, and roadside death markers, and hints of life lost along the highway with a blessing/prayer for the good passing of spirit. But Crow... Crow was more than a mass of flesh smashed into transition. Though crows live off roadside carrion and nonchalantly interact with 70 mph semis on a regular basis, they seldom are killed. They are smart and alert and, perhaps blessed with an aura of protection. I don't know, but the sight in the rearview mirror of my dear friend and guardian Crow destroyed and dead hit me like the jolt of some allegorical defibrillator and my heart cried out with a rush of silent ache, "Crow!" And, in that instant of extreme angst I burst free of the protection and suffocation of my father's muted being and felt the resurgence of sentiment and emotion charge through my essence and reassert my strange and wonderful identity.

And Carol, who isn't the least bit New-Age-ee or naive of reality, felt it just as clearly as if it had been her own soul zapped by the blessing of Crow dead upon the highway. Crow alive within my spirit. Crow who would depart the blood and feathers of the wet roadside and travel within me. She knew. And that evening, with tears and laughter and heartfelt sighs of relief, both she and Kristin repeatedly welcomed me home. "It's so good to have you back."

And in meditation where I speak to the Mystery like an old friend, I said to Crow, "I feel your feathery spirit. You're in here, aren't you?"

And Crow said, "For a while, or maybe for good. We'll see."

"Great. Now take me up. Fly me, Crow."

And in a voice you could imagine would come from such a tough old bird, Crow said, "You damned fool. You're afraid of heights."

"Oh, yeah."

And that's the way it would be for a couple more weeks until, almost as obsession, Carol and I made our way to the edge of the Grand Canyon and this amazing experience came to resolution.

My dad went on upon his *Great Journey*, bless him. He saved his boy, nearly destroyed his boy, and now may he find further purpose for his soul. Sister Nancy came to visit and we all had such a sweet and good time together. I hope she knows in my heart there was never a sense of family between Dad and Mom and me that was not completed by the essence of her love. And me? Well, I got to be as deeply sad and giddy and zany and holy as I had ever been. Yes.

It wasn't over, though.

And, of course, we did fly—my old buddy Crow and I.

Fear of heights is a fleshy matter: fear of falling, fear of smashing on the rocks, fear of making a fool of oneself with sniveling and clinging. Spirit knows nothing of such local folly. When Crow flew my spirit from front porch up over the lagoon and swept me on a great circle over the lake and then back out over the highway and the hotels and the cars and the beachcombers and with swoop through the spray of roiling surf and then up and up out above the great sea and higher and higher until with my arms and Crow's wings we embraced the entire world, there was nothing to fear but that possibly awe might swell so grand within my being I would explode into some dazzle-sparkling mist of galaxies and echoes of giddy rich laughter. Yeah, we flew, Crow and I.

And Carol might have asked, "Robert, what were you doing out on the porch?"

And I might have answered as I turned to her and blessed her with the *Smile* God had shimmered through the entire Universe to my eyes, "Oh, just taking it all in."

That's the way it could be again. Bless you, my father. Your stalwart soul saved me from despair. Now, sail on, good child of the daunting age of great wars and Great Depression. Release the desperation and violence of the century of your incarnation and let go. Let go.

Fly.

It was sometime in those weeks when visions of the Grand Canyon materialized in the imagination of our days.

We had planned a trip to Tucson to visit Carol's dear cousins, Tom and Bette, and over to Bullhead City to visit my old mountain buddy Russell and then on to Las Vegas to enjoy old friends. It was Carol who mentioned the Skywalk of Grand Canyon West.

The logistics of the trip were complex and brilliant. Carol stayed up most of an entire night studying schedules and maps and ended up with a combination of three flights and two car rentals that only pushed our expendable resources to the brink of bankruptcy, not quite over the edge.

With sheaves of Expedia.com printouts stuffed in carry-ons and fingers crossed we set out upon a journey to family and friends. But at the heart of it all, we set out, Carol, Robert, and the gruff and beautiful spirit of Crow, to stand upon a glass sidewalk that overhangs a 4000-foot abyss.

The last eight miles of the road out to the rim is dirt and not all that smooth. The night before a dusting of snow had left artful traces in the clefts of stone mountains and shady sides of eroded watercourses. It was a bright-sun cold November morning upon a high desert plateau, stark and marvelous.

As we crossed on to Hualapai tribal lands and neared the visitor center, I could feel a strange and powerful emotional energy rising within me—both exhilarating and deeply sad. In silence I drove the turning road, so self-absorbed that I didn't notice Carol was crying until she blew her nose.

With shaking words and lovely tears, she said, "Are you out here to let your father go?"

We both loved the old man.

"I don't think so. I think I've already pretty much done that. As much as I'm able. I really don't know why we've come, but, Man, it's a really big deal, isn't it?"

She nodded.

So many questions are never answered, but this one was. I couldn't be writing this if something hadn't come of this journey.

The Skywalk is an engineering marvel. The structure forms a horizontal arc that loops right out over the Grand Canyon. It would be cool just to walk out there and look over but add to this the fact that the floor and railings are made of glass. Wow! I mean when you step out there it's like walking on air where the first rock wall is 1300 feet down and then it falls on off another 3000 feet to the Colorado River at the bottom of the canyon. I told you I have a decent case of acrophobia, but somehow this was so far beyond standing on a roof or climbing one limb too high in a tree that all I felt was a thrilling sense of suspension. It was as if flesh and spirit found stasis upon that invisible plane upon which we stood. About us, scattered people chattered in a babble of languages, some giggling, some clearly terrified, some struck near silent in wonder. I am a poet and there was nothing I could say. Then in a rising rush of truth within me I realized the purpose for our being there. "Carol, I've come out here to let my old friend Crow free." And, with that, the feathery vision departed me. About us crows dropped deep into the chasm and then, with exhilarated caws ascended majestically upon the currents rising high above the earth-toned, shadow-sculpted, vast deep heart of a planet.

Carol and I stood there tear-streaked and filled with a liberating sense of loss and joy.

Oh, sadness, Crow is dead.

Oh, joy, Crow soars.

Oh, sadness, my father is dead.

Oh, joy, my father is free.

Oh, sadness, I have neither flesh of father nor feather of Crow to support me.

Oh, joy, I fly on alone...well, with a little help, of course.

Caw

It Is Your Time, My Friend
(And the time is now)

So...are you feeling better now?

Happy?

I know. Feedlot economies, greed-desiccated resources, imponderable dimensions, ubiquitous fear and death—just what you need to 'let the sun shine in and face it with a grin.'

Right?

I warned you this would not be easy. I think you would find little worth to a collection of drivel-and-glee aphorisms of sweetness and whoop-dee doo—you know, wit and wisdom from the painted smile of a clown. You've got some heavy burdens in your life and sometimes pain tells the morning and tears spill the day. Some of the phases of your life are hardly the stuff of grinning bliss. Your love leaves you, your kids think you're stupid, the latest tweaking of the economy has left you and a mob of other equally-skilled toilers out on the sidewalk in front of some corporate palace thinking about starting a new mid-life career in deep frying. (Remember how, during the Obama era of corporate bailouts, Ford Motor Company boasted that it needed no handout from the Fed? Oh, yeah, did they happen to mention that in the month or so before the crash of '08 they had laid off over thirty thousand employees? Thirty thousand middle-classed, vocationally ensconced participants in an industrial vision just tossed aside for the sake of rescuing the bottom dollar down at the stock store for the benefit of the financial elite.)

Man, stuff like that can suck the helium right out of your great big happy-faced balloon.

Maybe you don't know the song I quoted above:

> Let the sun shine in
> face it with a grin,

smilers never lose
and frowners never win.

Sure. Tell Dick Cheney that frowners never win.

No, it's not easy to be happy—not if you're living with your eyes open, your mind attuned to reality, your heart willing to risk a little compassion.

It's risky being truly alive in a dangerous world. But, and perhaps this is the point of this whole book: who wants to live a life hunkered down in some suffocating bunker of blindness, delusion, and selfishness? Not me.

Being happy has nothing to do with being numb.

Living a useful life has nothing to do with living a safe life. There is no safety in the assurances of culture and society. We are on our own, all of us. And aside from the fact that nobody really wants to listen to our whining, we must all quit bitching and know that most days can be retrieved from gloom and doom. Cynicism sucks!

Look, we've dealt with:

Fear—laughter, hope, and beauty.

Infinite insignificance—cosmic flowers and the existence of an amazing sentient marvel called you.

Finite time in the local feedlot—nobody owns your soul, your love, or the free-range wildness of your laughter.

The daunting physics of a gazillion dimensions of ever—it isn't what our humble senses can perceive that is the measure of our world. It is the amazing reach of what we can feel that tells our essence.

Mortal frailty—love and art kick mortal butt.

Mortal finality—*CAW!* And how the spirit may fly.

And the secret? Yes, the secret. Every book has a secret to tell. Actually it is the nature of art. Art does not keep secrets; it tells them. This simple truth was lost to a couple of generations of 'inside joke' charlatan artists who throughout the past century filled art galleries and concert halls and artsy magazines with obscurity, noise, and ego mumble. Nonsense! It's this simple—if you don't get it, then, for you, it isn't art. If art's forms and patterns, singing sentiments, and whisper-shouted nuance and roar leave you feeling inept, stupid, left out; art failed.

I heard a story once about a famous Italian opera composer, I think it was Giuseppe Verdi, who was traveling with an entourage through the countryside when a group of field hands recognized him and blocked the road. To get the full effect here, imagine it is late afternoon in Tuscany and the sunlight is golden upon the verdant hillsides and the men are ruddy and glistening with the perspiration of their noble toil.

"Maestro! Maestro!," they shouted. And then, in full operatic fervor, *en masse* they sang for him a grand chorus from one of his operas.

Wow.

You see, they got the secret of the art.

I've told you my tales. I've rambled and raved my thoughts, I've given my art and now, let me be certain that you get my secret.

Here it is:

We must participate in our own happiness.

Uncle Bob isn't happy when he's sitting on his hinder watching serial killer, autopsy reruns of *Miami Guts* or the contrived competition of marginally talented performers on television. Uncle Bob needs to get out of his recliner and not passively watch *Dancing Celebs* on the screen, but grab his love Carol and dance madly about the living room like the bliss-crazed fool that he is.

Get it? The ideas are here for you, the concepts are in place, the ink of my poetry has flowed upon the page for you to know.

Now it's time to take action yourself.

You know—play a game of tag, giggle with a child, let yourself know the night-shimmer blessing of starlight, dance and sing about your kitchen as you season sustenance with love.

Did you know that a banjo is an open-tuned instrument? This means that when you pick it up and just strum your fingers across the strings you are playing a complete chord—and that single

165

chord is the beginning of thousands of songs. Thousands. Hey, that's easier than turning on a radio.

If you don't happen to have a banjo handy (that's hard for me to imagine, but I guess some of you are truly deprived), go down to the local music store and try one out. I'll get you started here and then you can make your own way to the *Grand Ole Opry*.

Okay, ready? Now just give the open strings a good strum. Don't be self-conscious—that's what I have been throughout my life and have ended up singing most of my masterful lyrics and plunking my intricate melodies to my big sleepy dog, Jesse. Forget that the clerk is likely a virtuoso, plunk-wild dazzler and just let yourself go. Strum confidently the full rich G-chord that has been waiting there as potential energy locked up in this instrument dying for you to release it to be heard. Listen to the beautiful music you have made and then sing out with heart unbound:

Flies in the buttermilk
two by two.

Then, just smile an honest smile, hang the banjo back on the wall, and walk proudly from the store and on out into the whole wide world as a person actively participating in the creation and proliferation of your own joy.

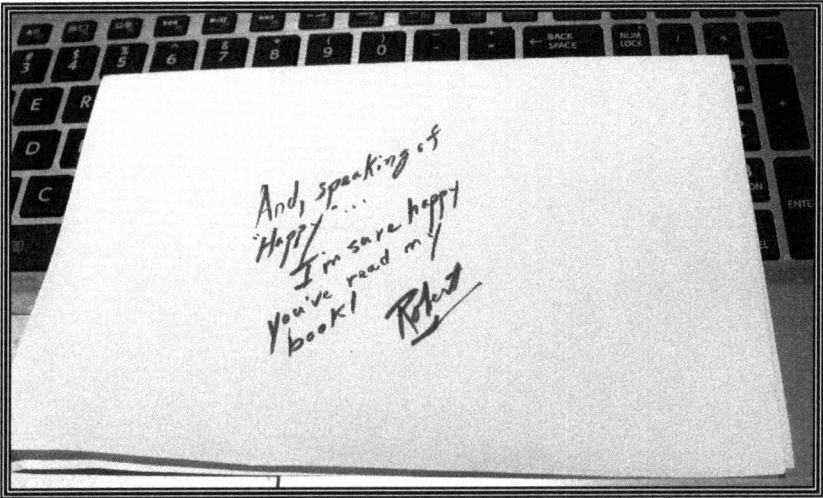

And, speaking of "Happy"... I'm sure happy you've read my book! Robert

Other Works by Robert Nichols

Books etc.

The Kristin Book, 1987**.** Story of the first fifteen years of the life of my daughter who was born with Down Syndrome.

This book, reissued with an update, is now available in eBook format as *The Kristin Book: Update 2013.* It is available on a variety of eBook readers.

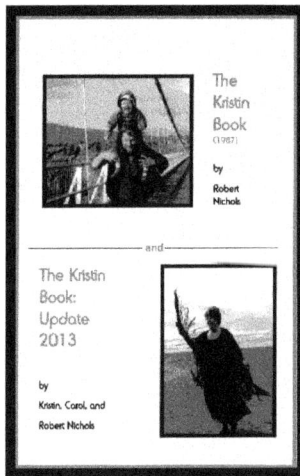

Take the Aspen Train, 1988. Co-authored with Edward Larsh. Coffee table, Colorado history / social philosophy / train book. *(No longer available)*

Adventures in the High Wind, 1990. Collection of my poems, stories, and essays.
   eBook edition, 2013.
   Available on a variety of eBook readers,.

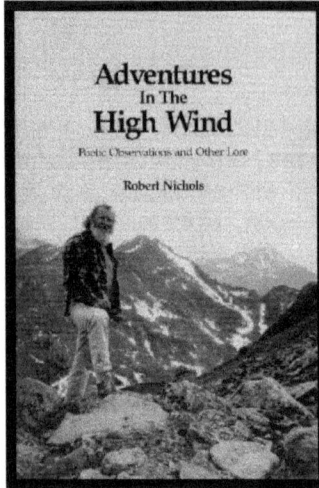

Leadville, USA, 1993. Co-authored with Edward Larsh. Oral history of Leadville, Colorado. *(No longer available)*

The High Priest of Hallelujah, 1999. Niche-less novel of poetic vision, humor, and satire.
   eBook edition, 2015.

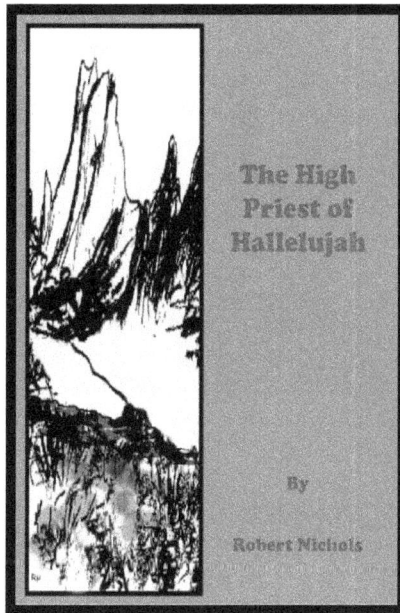

The High
Priest of
Hallelujah

By

Robert Nichols

Summer Words, 2000, 2001. Collection of short essays about laughter, God, knife throwing and much more.

e-Book edition, 2014.

Available on a variety of eBook readers.

The Booklets, 2001 and... 12-14 page booklets of poetry, short stories, essays—you know: literature. Currently there are five of these little gems published with more to come.

The Five Great Truths of Uncle Bob, 2002. A culminating work of philosophy, religion, and practical wisdom (and all on one side of a sheet of paper).

God of the Poets, 2003. It took me twenty years to get this one right. When I finished the first version in '83 I didn't know enough to write my own novel. Perhaps now I do. I was pretty much just a stenographer for the real author, God. This isn't traditional stuff. It's a story of art, love, humanity and...*the purpose of life*.

e-Book edition, 2014.

Available on a variety of eBook readers.

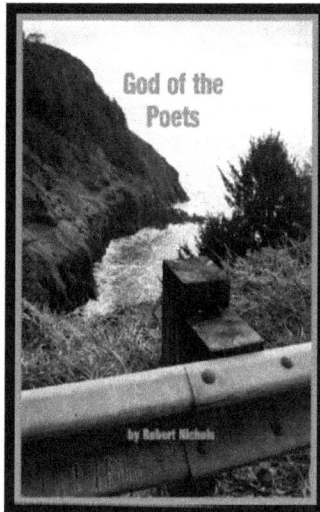

Albatross: The Curse of Honesty, eBook 2013. The first novel I wrote, and re-wrote, and finally published as an e-Book. It's a funny and touching tale of a fellow whose life is nearly destoyed by the curse of absolute honesty.

Available on a variety of eBook readers.

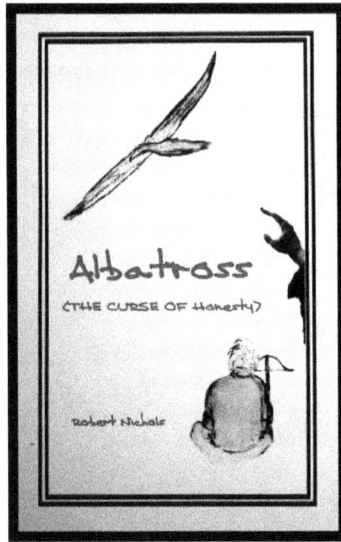

The Great Book of Bob, 2009.
The Great Book of Bob **eBook edition**, 2014.

A unified collection of humorous, soul-wrenching, and harshly honest tales and thoughts gleaned from a lifelong love story— stories of a poet's love of sunrises, poetic epiphanies, laughter, and for the soulmate of his life. And the best part about it, it's not some icky-sticky, lovey-poo bunch of hearts and flowers. It's hard-edged wonder and real reason for all of us to be glad to be alive. I tell *my* stories that we may each realize the significance of our own.

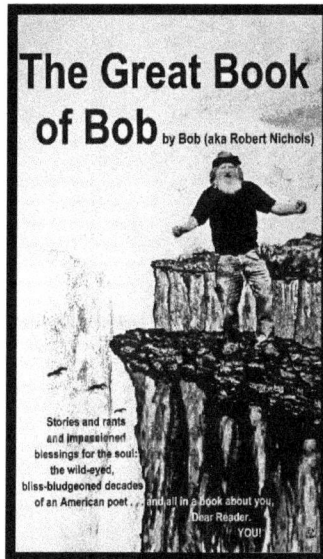

The Great Book of Bob by Bob (aka Robert Nichols)

Stories and rants and impassioned blessings for the soul: the wild-eyed, bliss-bludgeoned decades of an American poet... and all in a book about you, Dear Reader. YOU!

THE FOOTLOCKER SERIES

This is a series of eBooks gleaned from fifty years of writing excavated from Robert Nichols' old footlocker of notebooks and scrap papers—the repository of a life of art.

Limited, spiral-bound print editions are available at this time. Contact Robert Nichols / P.O. Box 406; Lincoln City, Oregon 97367.

about Time: Poems and Other Stories

The first in the series—poetry, stories, and photography about ancient time, the time of children, the time of young adults, and the time of growing old. It's really not about time at all. This is a book about life.

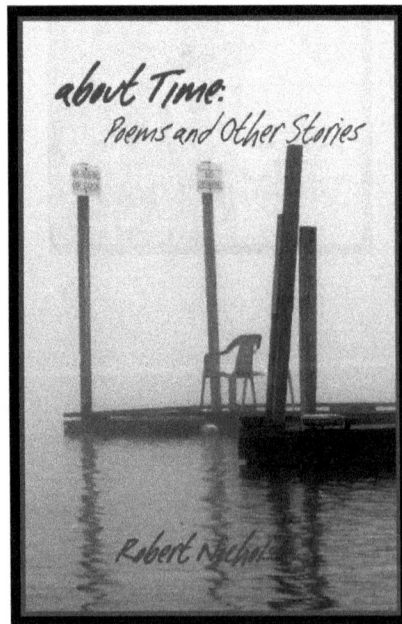

about Mountain Living: Finding a Way *(2015)*

Poetry and stories from Robert Nichols' years in the high country of Colorado. A harsh/sweet journey of flesh and spirit.

about Seasons—the Wind and Weather of Our Days (2016)

Poems of the Seasons—not just some cliché sweetness about leaves and blossoms either. This is the core stuff of being. Seasons, wind, and weather—the fierce and beautiful power of Nature that can keep us humble and exhilarated throughout our lives. It is the very "life and death" intensity of these metamorphic cycles that excites the turning of our years with risk and wonder. Time takes away our days, storms wash away our safety, seasons etch our flesh with danger. Old Spirits out on the plains once told me, "Earth shall never be tame...celebrate your fear and feel you are alive!" Yes!

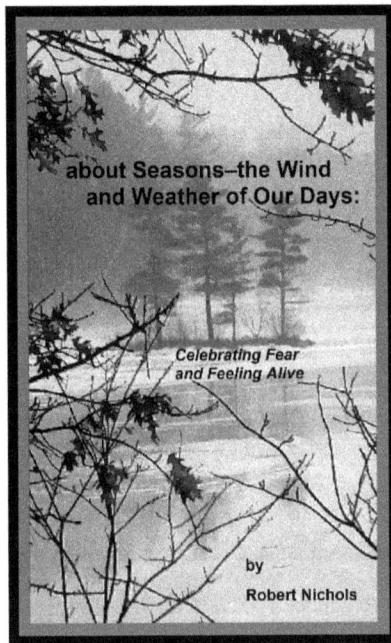

about Seasons—the Wind and Weather of Our Days:

Celebrating Fear and Feeling Alive

by

Robert Nichols

Robert Nichols—former school teacher, carpenter,
truck driver, factory worker, Maytag Man, etc.—
is a poet, novelist, essayist,
impromptu philosopher
who writes, carves, sings,
and loves life with his family in Oregon

Happiness: A Family Selfie
2015
Carol, Kristin, Robert
and
the Strange Little Dog, Molly